Officers & Gentlemen

Officers & Gentlemen

Two accounts of
British Officers During
the Peninsular War

Officer of Light Dragoons
by Peter Hawker

Campaigns in
Portugal and Spain
by William Graham

LEONAUR

Officers & Gentlemen: Two Accounts of
British Officers During the Peninsula War
Officer of Light Dragoons by Peter Hawker
Campaign in Portugal and Spain by William Graham

First published under the titles
Journal of a Regimental Officer
and
Travels through Portugal and Spain
During the Peninsula War

Leonaur is an imprint
of Oakpast Ltd

Copyright in this form © 2009 Oakpast Ltd

ISBN: 978-1-84677-638-0 (hardcover)
ISBN: 978-1-84677-637-3 (softcover)

http://www.leonaur.com

Contents

Officer of Light Dragoons

Peter Hawker

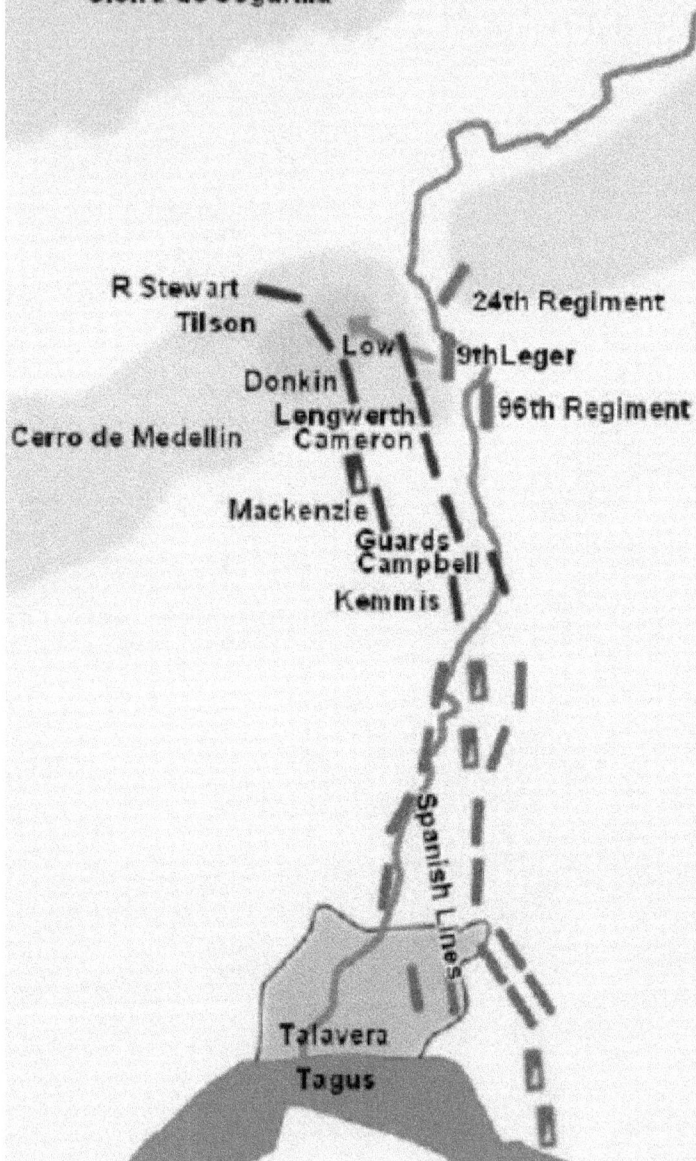

Sierra de Segurilla

R Stewart
Tilson
Low
24th Regiment
9thLeger
Donkin
Lengwerth
96th Regiment
Cameron
Cerro de Medellin
Mackenzie
Guards
Campbell
Kemmis
Spanish Lines
Talavera
Tagus

Contents

"—— quantus equis quantus adest viris Sudor!"
Morage.

Advertisement

The contents of the following pages (never intended for the public eye) were hastily noted down amidst the scenes attempted to be delineated; and the author's sufferings from a wound have precluded him the possibility of afterwards correcting them.

This candid statement will, it is hoped, plead for inaccuracies and frivolous incidents; and those persons who are most able to criticise will no doubt have the liberality to consider the disadvantages under which this narrative makes its appearance.

The intervening dates omitted throughout the *Journal* are those only on which there occurred neither change of place nor circumstances.

Journal of an Officer

1808. *November 19*,—Left town to join my regiment, which was on the march for Falmouth, and ordered to halt at Exeter and adjacent places. On the 21st arrived at Tiverton, the station of my squadron; where it remained till the 29th, when, agreeably to a route received the preceding evening, we marched as follows:— The above day to Crediton; 30th, to Oakhampton; December the 1st, to Launceston; 2nd, to Bodmin; 3rd, to Truro; and on the 4th arrived at Falmouth, and immediately commenced embarkation from the quay. We were soon on board, and sailed out to the middle of the harbour, to remain at anchor till further orders. The transport (a *ci-de-vant* collier[1]) in which it was my lot to be stowed, was about the dirtiest in the fleet, from the slovenly and drunken habits of her master, who, to do him justice, I think approached nearer to the ursine breed than any of his floating fraternity. With this edifying messmate I remained till the 15th; when, at seven a. m., a signal for sailing was hoisted; and at twelve the whole fleet got under weigh with a fair wind. After clearing land, the commodore made signal that the empty ships attached to our convoy were bound for Vigo, and we for the Tagus. This was the first official intelligence we received of our destination.

17th.—Entered the Bay of Biscay, going at the rate of nine knots an hour.

---

1. She was then scarcely sea-worthy; very soon after sprung a leak, and was discharged the service at unsafe.

19th. —Towards five p. m, we had to weather a very severe gale, accompanied with showers of hail, which drove us violently, and considerably damaged, our rigging. Towards dusk it rather abated. From the darkness and repeated squalls, during the night we lost our convoy. We however, regained it early in the morning.

20th.—About four p. m. made the Burlings (a cluster of small islands about forty miles from the Rock of Lisbon), when signal was made for lying-to. We there continued beating about till next morning. It blew very hard, attended with an extremely high sea, which made the ship labour so much that it was impossible to stand, or even lie in our births without danger of getting our heads broke. We were rolled from side to side with the greatest violence, and without a moment's intermission. This, together with the continual creaking of the ship, the stifled state we were in by having our dead-lights up and being without air, added to the effluvia and suffocation of a smoking chimney, kept us the whole night in the very essence of misery.

21st—At six a. m. we got under sail, and at twelve came in full view of the Rock of Lisbon. The villages interspersed on the sides of this grand promontory, with the serrated summits of the rocks, many of which are crowned with churches and towers, form a novel and truly interesting scene. About two we entered the Tagus, with a steady breeze; and having passed the fort and castle of St. Julian, the City of Lisbon opened to our view in all its splendour. The day being remarkably fine heightened the beauties of the scene, while the British fleet in the fore-ground gave a finish to the picture. At five came to anchor about half a mile from the town, where we waited for orders.

24th.—At half past four in the afternoon we began to disembark, and it was dusk before we marched off. We proceeded to Belem, a suburb of Lisbon four miles from the Quay.

When we arrived there it was quite dark. The confusion and scramble that ensued in the streets for forage and provision, where neither English nor Portuguese could understand each other, may be easily conceived. The men went to the barracks at this place, and the officers were, served with billets on private houses; but some days elapsed before we could find out the *Dons* on whom our company was to be inflicted. In the interim, we were forced to lay down where we could, many officers taking up their quarters under their horses,

This being Christmas eve, I went at midnight to visit the convent of St. Jeronimo. Although no advocate for the pomp and ostentation of Popish ceremonials, the service was performed with so much solemnity that it was impossible entirely to withhold admiration. The organ was peculiarly fine, and in very good hands: the friar who played it evinced the greatest skill in his performance of the anthems. The architecture of the convent is considered a master-piece of the kind; but being night, my view was confined to the interior decorations.

28th.—Went to the play at Lisbon. The theatre is in every respect inferior to those of our own metropolis. The entertainments of the evening consisted of a comedy, which was performed with a great deal of low buffoonery, followed by a ballet. The dancers, both male and female, displayed great agility and strength of muscle; but of the materials required to captivate they were certainly not in possession; gracefulness was here very deficient.

The scenery was wretched in the extreme. The most I can say in favour of the performance must he bestowed on the orchestra; as the few musicians who composed it played with more attention and expression than our London fiddlers, who emphatically call themselves professors of music.

29th.—Rode to the grand aqueduct, which, with the scenery around, and the extensive prospect it commands, afforded ample gratification for the bad roads and stony hills I had to ascend. The oranges and lemons hung so conveniently, that I had only to pluck them when thirsty, without the trouble of dismounting.

30th.—The army received instructions to march; and our

first division was ordered to advance the succeeding morning, on its way to the frontiers; but this was countermanded before night.

31st.—Went to the Italian opera at St Carlos, which is considered the most fashionable entertainment in Lisbon. The house is good, but in point of decoration is inferior to ours. The orchestra department, consisting of about forty musicians was most ably conducted; but the singing was far short of what I had been led to expect. The vocal performers displayed no execution, and, with the exception of two or three leading characters, were equally deficient in taste and expression. The disciples of Terpsichore, so far as nature was concerned, were extremely awkward; and though I allow their dancing to be very good, yet their thick ankles and robust limbs rather excited laughter than admiration. But their *chef d'œuvre* compensated for all defects: I mean, their style of action in the ballet, which was graceful and expressive.

1809. *January 2nd.*—This morning I devoted to the inspection of Belem palace, formerly one of the most splendid royal residences in Europe. It has been sadly altered within a few months: the French have not only stripped it of every picture and ornament at all portable, but mutilated the very walls, in their rapacious efforts to rob them of all that was valuable. Only two inferior rooms, and a small chapel, remain in any tolerable repair. A variety of packages lay scattered about the hall, which Junot in his hurry, had not time to dispatch they chiefly contained precious marbles, and sculpture of most excellent workmanship. The gardens, which are magnificent, and ornamented by masterly pieces of statuary, could formerly boast of one of the finest aviaries. The building indeed remains, but its motley-feathered tenantry (collected from every quarter of the globe) are nearly extirpated.

The greatest havoc was made among them by a puppy named Beauharnois (of course one, of the Napoleon dynasty), who resided here sometime, and during his stay had the aviary put in requisition, not to gratify his eye or his ear, but his gluttonous appetite: his favourite relish was a canary, and he was every morning, for his breakfast, served with about a dozen of these unfortunate finches. It appeared, however, he had a fellow-feeling for birds of prey, as the vultures, and the whole of the falcon tribe, have continued unmolested. There are also remaining some wild beasts, which the French seem to have treated with equal respect.

9th.—Having procured an interpreter, I, with a party, crossed the Tagus. We landed in Port Brandon, opposite Belem Castle. Nearly four miles up the road, there is a tract of wood, about eight leagues in circumference, called the King's Forest. We had made this excursion for a day's sport with the Portuguese game, hearing that the forest abounded with red-legged partridges and woodcocks, and knowing that it formerly was one of the Prince Regent's favourite beats when he went for a *grande chasse*. We, however, found nothing the whole day but a few rabbits, and returned without getting a shot. In the course of our walk, we passed several plants which had been grubbed up, and discovered many places where wild boars had lately been. Notwithstanding our game-bags were empty, we returned pleased with the excursion, as the scenery made amends for our bad sport.

This wood is entirely composed of evergreens and short aromatic shrubs. The ground being hilly, you sometimes, by getting on an eminence, see over miles of the forest; but your extensive prospect, being over a continued region of firs, is one dark green, gradually fading, from distance, to a dim blue.

10th.—Visited the museum at Belem, which contains an extensive collection in natural history. It was principally founded by the Prince Regent, and has attached to it an excellent botanic garden. This museum is divided into two large apartments: the first contains a valuable collection of minerals, in which the finest specimens of all the Brasilian and other precious stones are to be found, as well as a great variety of fossils. This leads to the second, which is filled with beasts, birds, insects, and fishes, in high preservation, with a beautiful collection of shells[2].

11th.—Our regiment received orders to re-embark; and, on the evening of the 12th, marched for that purpose to Lisbon; where, in consequence of being unable to get the detachment on board, we lay at picquet all night in a stable.

13th.—At seven in the morning we commenced embarkation; and it was above two hours before we were on board, as the vessel lay far off in the harbour, and our horses were conveyed to her in boats.

14th.—The instructions were recalled, and the *Nautilus*, sent off with dispatches: we therefore remained at anchor without a commodore, and totally ignorant of our destination,

24th.—Returned on shore, and went with a large party on an excursion to the Rock of Lisbon, which is about four leagues beyond Belem. After being driven in a *caliche* for near five hours, at the rate of Russell's *Exeter Fly*, we reached the town of Cintra,—I must not forget to revert to the neat appearance of the roads we had passed; which, with the exception of places out of repair, were regularly paved like a street; fenced on both sides with hedges of the most beautiful geraniums; and surrounded, in every direction, by what in England would be considered the choicest exotics,—They are in unison with the paradise to which they lead!

To describe the environs of Cintra would be a task for which I have unfortunately neither time nor abilities. The Rock itself would claim a volume, on the variety of its ancient monuments; and the views around require the pencil of a first-rate artist,

Having taken some refreshment, and hired asses, we proceeded to the Rock. The structure of the convent of Pina, and the Moorish castle upon the very pinnacle of this stupendous height, add to its scenery the most terrific grandeur; and the serrated summits, shooting up like crystals, are about two thou-

---

2. Soon, after, all these things were packed up, to be sent to the Brazils; it being thought that the British were about to evacuate the country.

sand four hundred feet, nearly perpendicular, from the sea. The ponderous cliffs stand one upon another with the appearance of every moment falling; and their broken masses threaten destruction to the traveller. An ancient Moorish castle, constructed on this rock, has the same awful look; and is so built, that the walls and towers are carried from one of these massive stones, sixty yards in girth, to another. Having surveyed these, we sallied forth on our Jerusalem ponies to ascend the Passes, and to arrive at the convent and castle.—The safety and agility with which the donkeys climb up the hills and scramble through the stones is scarcely to be credited.

Having performed our tedious and fatiguing ascent, we reached the convent of Pina, through which we were conducted by an old friar, whose venerable look gave the cloisters additional solemnity. This place is remarkable for its plainness; and the occupiers, unlike most of their monastic brethren, seem to have no earthly treasure to boast of we saw no one but our guide, although, in the refectory, there were covers laid for fourteen.

The Moorish Castle next attracted our attention. Its situation is equally romantic with that of the convent. The structure is rude; but in some of the towers we could plainly discern the remains of paintings on the stones. There are still, in tolerable preservation, a multiplicity of ancient monuments, and many with inscriptions in Moorish characters. We had scarcely finished our inspection, when a very thick fog came on: indeed we had been some time in the clouds when first we reached Pina, as a mist enveloped us before we had half way ascended the height. We descended by the same pass, and soon reached a clear atmosphere. A grand scene then presented itself in different features, the fog having obscured the greater part of its majestic eminences. Our view was therefore circumscribed by orange, lemon, and other fruit trees, with which its bases were encircled. Evergreens of all kinds are seen intersecting the rocks, and shooting from the fissures to their very summits. Aromatic exhalations from various shrubs, and the foliage of innumerable vines, are everywhere presented, and exhibit a vegetation peculiar to this luxuriant garden of nature.

Having thus agreeably passed our time till late in the evening, we returned to the inn, where an excellent dinner had been waiting our arrival. Everything was served up in the British style; as Madam Cavigioli, our landlady, although married to an Italian, was an Irish woman, The landlord and his brother attended us during dinner, and afterwards amused us cheerfully with vocal and instrumental music. We then returned to our beds, which were the more agreeable from being in the English fashion.

25th.—Waking early in the morning, the prospect from the window even exceeded my expectations; the town of Cintra under our hotel, and the verdure of the plains fading to an air tint, was one of the richest scenes. The clouds gradually uncapping the distant heights, and leaving their purple heads, contrasted with the opening dawn, contributed to the scene more than sublunary beauties.

Our party soon sallied forth with their sketch-books; and made the most of this fine opportunity to collect some landscapes. We passed orchards where the boughs were breaking down with fruit, and the lemons dropping into the rivulets that flanked the road: we entered one grove, which, in many places, was ankle deep with the. fruit that lay mouldering in the path.

Having been busily employed for several hours, we were compelled to leave this place without thoroughly exploring its beauties. The hour we had to spare was dedicated to the palace of the Prince Regent, latterly the country residence of Junot, and the house where the *Convention* of Cintra was signed.

The building is modern; and one of the best constructed in Portugal. From the front you look through groves upon the rocks, and the sight is rather contracted; but the back part brings you to a sudden descent, and stands so high above everything in that direction, as to afford one of the most extensive prospects in the country: the sea appears to the left, and the convent of Maffra far in the back ground to the right Finding that we had been tempted to trespass on our time, we hastened to the inn; ordered the vehicles and mules; and reluctantly returned to our floating dungeons.

25th.—The horses having become sickly from being, so long stored on shipboard, we were ordered to disembark, and take up our former quarters; till further instructions were sent to the commander in chief; and on the 28th the regiment was all landed.

February 28th.—Orders were issued for the army to hold itself in readiness to march;—the heavy baggage to be sent on board the store-ships;—and every preparation to be made for advancing towards the frontiers.

March 3rd.—Two squadrons of dragoons were ordered to march on the advance; but in the evening a countermand arrived.

4th.—The order of the 3rd was renewed;—and on the 5th, the first and fourth squadrons proceeded to Loaires.

The two squadrons, of the regiment being divided into four, each troop branched off in a different direction, leaving Loaires for the second and third squadrons, which marched in on the 6th and formed the headquarter division. I went to Bucellas, about a league and a half in front. This was the advanced post, occupied by about eighty dragoons and a half-brigade of German artillery. On our entering this village, we found that the serjeant who had been sent on for billets had never arrived; and in consequence a regular scramble took place. To complete our difficulties, not a soul in the place could speak any language but his own, in which we were altogether deficient.

However, by making signs, with the assistance of a little main force, we put up the men and horses. We had then to look out for ourselves, and got into some empty houses without windows; and having had no breakfast, commenced an attack on the produce of the village, which consisted only of musty eggs, ill-cured bacon, and bad cheese. These we washed down with some liquor called wine, which as vinegar was certainly good. However, when the natives found that we most unfashionably paid for things, they produced some real Bucellas, which, as a summer wine, was excellent. We drank it at two *vintims* (about three-pence) per quart.

Having noted our arrival, I must revert to our two days' march.

On entering Loaires, we were well received, and tolerably provided for. The above place stands in a flat, and is considered unhealthy: its appearance and situation, however, are pretty; and its soil produces the finest oranges. Being within two leagues of Lisbon, it is (unlike most of the Portuguese villages) supplied with the necessaries of life, and contains several shops, with a good *caza de comer* (or eating-house)—which, by the way, was not discovered till we had made every preparation for cooking our own dinners.

On leaving Loaires half a league, we came to a neat village, called St. Antonio de Tojal, where a great part of the houses surround a large green. This leads to the convent and gardens, for which this place is celebrated.

On departing from Tojal, you ascend from the valley, and leave a village to the right, passing between two immense chains of hills. Within a mile of Bucellas, the one on the left bears away for Cabeça de Monta Chique; and the other continues farther, and takes nearly an opposite direction; both commanding the low countries, and forming a very strong position. The hills on the right are divided from the pass by a deep ravine, which in the rainy season is so increased, that the water is forced in torrents against its rugged sides, and forms a sort of cascade for several miles.

7th.—A party of us went out with guns, accompanied by a priest, who, as far as we could understand him, promised to shew us plenty of game. We saw nothing all day but one hare[3], and returned quite fatigued, inviting his Reverence to dinner; who so readily agreed to attack our mutton, that I suspect he made the shooting party only with that intention.

11th.—We made a second attempt; and hired a bandy-legged fellow, who was considered the Nimrod of the place, and kept

---

3. The hares of Portugal are about the size of ours: their fur is much longer, and in some .parts darker: they have a great deal of white in the fore-quarters.

two hounds. These animals were broken-in to draw on birds; and though they never came to a dead point, they gave the shooter plenty of time to get up. We, however, had our usual bad sport. Though we found about twelve partridges, the weather was so stormy, they were the whole day on the run, and, in spite of every manoeuvre, we could not even get a snap-shot.—Our *chasse* ended in the destruction of a Portuguese owl, which flew from under a heap of stones. This bird was scarcely bigger than a field fare: its eyes were immensely large, and of a fine bright yellow: in plumage it nearly resembled our common brown owl. It ran nearly as fast as a partridge, and flew like a woodpecker.

In the evening we went out with our casting nets, but all the stream appeared to contain was a few small fish, like bleak.

April 3rd.—The out-posts being relieved, our division marched into Loaires.

6th.—The army received orders to commence its march towards Oporto; which was then occupied by the enemy's troops under Marshal Soult.

7th.—Rode over to Lisbon, to equip myself for campaigning. Hurried as I was, I had resolved not to take my leave of this place without having seen its greatest curiosity. I allude to the inner chapel of St. Roqoue's Church, of which I regretted not having time to make a regular inspection. The richness of it is a true emblem of Roman Catholic pomp. The pillars, from top to bottom of the chapel, are of *lapis lazuli* and amethyst, set, apparently, in fine gold. One of the altars is composed of amethyst, alabaster, and coral, combined with the most valuable minerals that an unlimited expense through the world could procure. There is another, worked in a mass of silver, and carved to represent angels, &c. which the guide informed me cost seven thousand pounds. The candlesticks belonging to it are said to be of double that value.—This temple, instead of common stone, is paved with the choicest mosaic; and three large Scripture pieces, which struck me as most valuable and masterly paintings, on my having a ladder brought, and inspecting them, proved to be entirely composed of the mosaic work

It may perhaps be unnecessary to add, that Mr. Junot had had these packed up, for the grand receptacle of all plunder. His interception here must have occasioned extreme disappointment, as the collections for this church are said to have cost three millions of crusades.

9th.—The regiment commenced its march, and the head-quarter division advanced to Sobral. When the troops entered this place, the confusion exceeded everything we had before experienced. The town, which was scarcely large enough to put up half a regiment, was crammed with six thousand infantry, in addition to the staff, and our own two squadrons. The cavalry officers were left adrift, to lie down how they could—A large party of us walked into a house, where we immediately began foraging; and at last made up so comfort-a picnic, that we invited three friends to dinner. We had scarcely sat down, when we were invaded by one hundred and fifty soldiers, who were quartered on the same house. They were all packed into one room over our heads, and we were in momentary expectation of having them through the ceiling.

We were, however, soon relieved from our post of danger, by getting turned out of the billet. Everyone then walked off, with his victuals in one hand and saddle-bags in the other, in search of a floor where he could lie down in peace. I separated from my companions, and got into the house of a poor man; the whole of whose mansion consisted of two bad rooms, a little kitchen, and a pigsty, joined together under so thin a roof that daylight appeared through in several places.

The troops were directed to remain in Sobral till further orders, and with a fair prospect of short commons, as very soon after their first arrival not a bit of bread was to be bought.

11th.—A detachment of our regiment was ordered out to a hamlet called Xam, to make room for the artillery. I had the fortune to be one of those emancipated from head-quarters, and proceeded to this place. It was so small it could only contain the third of a troop; and we were obliged to have the greater part of the men scattered over the country, in straggling huts.

Xam is situated in a green valley. Contiguous to it stands a *quinta*[4], which, of course, we selected for ourselves and myrmidons. The man left in charge of the house, thinking his master's absence a good excuse to refuse us admission, would not give up the keys, till we had recourse to the never-failing remedy of beginning to storm his doors. He then very politely produced them; and gave us up five rooms and a kitchen, with a good stable; and conducted us to a large garden of fruit and vegetables. Our only difficulty then was, to get at the crockery; as we had scarcely anything to use, and our deputy host, with the usual embraces and palaver of a Portuguese, declared he had produced the whole contents of the house: but, meeting with a large cupboard, and slipping back the bolt with a sabre, we discovered two services of china, with plenty of glass and everything requisite, besides sugar, honey, and other articles of provision.

12th.—When sitting comfortably down to breakfast, we observed we were too well off, to remain long in these quarters— though indeed, at the time. We thought the army would not advance for ten days. In a few minutes after, a route came for us to march at one o'clock in the afternoon. We accordingly took leave of our comforts, and went off to Arneiro.

13th.—Marched to Cadaval and Vermilha, passing Villa Verda. The road here, being among broken rocks, is in many places scarcely passable. In descending the heights, the views are beautiful; and on getting into the valley, the appearance of the rear troops had a pretty effect, from the serpentine direction of the passes they were coming down. On our left was Vimiera and Torres Vedras; and to our right stood a stupendous mountain, which we had seen for three days.

14th.—The army proceeded on the advance. The country in this day's march was dreary and barren, and the views, though

---

4. Gentleman's country seat.

very extensive, not so picturesque. We were struck with the majestic appearance of the Burlings, against, which we could plainly discern the bursting of a tremendous surge.—The town of Obidos, with its ancient Moorish fortifications, had a fine effect from the hills by which we entered it. The church stood so near the road, we had just time to dismount and run in: it is of a hexagonal form, and, though not to be named after St Roque's, contained many ornaments of considerable value.

After descending from the strong position of Obidos to a vale, and advancing half a league, we reached Caldos; where the army halted, and awaited the arrival of the commander in chief.— Caldos is a very large town, and was certainly the cleanest and neatest of any we had then seen in Portugal. In this place there is a house with several warm baths, which, I was informed, are similar to those at Harrowgate. Here is also a temporary amphitheatre, of many years' standing, which the natives told me was still used for bull-fights.

16th,—Marched for Alcobaça; to which, which, the exception of a few rough passes on the sides of hills, we found the road very good, being sandy, broad, and well calculated for the march of cavalry. The scenery around us afforded a pleasing variety. On our arrival in Alcobaça, the inhabitants were: drawn up on each side of the street, where men, women, and children, were shouting with exclamations of joy, and crying "*viva, viva!*" accompanied by the ringing of bells, waving of handkerchiefs, and every other mark of exultation.

After getting billeted off, we hastened to the convent of Santo Bernardo, which is the largest in Portugal, and the sepulchre of many kings. The apartments here are very extensive; but, instead of fine pictures, of which they are worthy, they are hung round with daubs that would do little credit to a sign-painter,

The chapel, though perhaps not intrinsically so valuable as St. Roque's, is apparently far more splendid. This edifice is formed like a cross, and the whole of its inside embellished with the finest carving, which, being entirely covered with gilding, has a, most magnificent appearance. There are two organs, opposite each other, which are decorated with sculpture, and richly gilded, and have pipes made like trumpets, projecting horizontally, so as to throw out the sound and produce a very powerful tone. Among the monuments, there are two of particularly fine workmanship, and each of them is supported by six lions couchant carved in stone.

The library next attracted our notice. It is sixty paces in length, and fourteen in breadth. The ornaments here display exquisite taste; and, though not so rich as the chapel, this apartment has so light and neat an effect, that we gave it a decided preference. It is paved with a variety of marble; and, before a selection of the most valuable volumes was sent on ship-board, was entirely filled with books.

The next thing to be seen was the kitchen, which is immensely large, and has a canal running through it. The water is forced by a wheel with great rapidity, for the purpose of more hastily washing the cooking utensils. A grand dinner is dressed here daily for the friars, to which all generals, staff and field officers, had a regular invitation during their stay; and, indeed, any officer-who chose to go, was hospitably received.

Having surveyed the convent, we repaired to our billet. We were here extremely fortunate in our host, who received us with the greatest hospitality, and, as well as he could express himself, begged that during our residence in his house we would consider everything it afforded as our own. He insisted on our coming to every meal at his table, and gave orders for all our servants to be well entertained in the kitchen. Our *Don's* style of living was sumptuous: we commenced with an elegant dinner, and (what is not always the case) continued to partake of one equally good every day.—Although our host was unable to converse with us, he contrived to keep us constantly amused; particularly those fond of music; he played the piano and guitar, and had great taste in singing. In order to promote a conference, the apothecary of Alcobaça, who spoke French, was invited to spend the afternoon, and requested to act as interpreter.

This was one of the drollest fellows we had met with: he kept us in a roar of laughter all dinnertime. Indeed, his very look was enough to promote mirth:—he had a constant smile on his face, which was embellished with a nose and chin nearly meeting, though between them he could just conveniently pass a walnut. The cut of his coat, and general appearance, was completed by a tremendous periwig; the *summit* of which was capped, *à la pictoresque,* with a triangular, cocked hat—Our landlord seemed so delighted at seeing the party thus entertained, that he gave him an invitation to meet us every day at dinner, which the doctor most readily accepted.

17th, 18th, and 19th.—Our good host gave routs, inviting all his neighbours to meet us. After tea and coffee, we had music, vocal and instrumental; with cards; followed by a pleasant dance; and concluding with a hot supper, where our friend the doctor was in great force.

20th.—Walked round the estate of our landlord, and took some luncheon with a friar, at his house in the wood. With other things, he gave us some delicious wine: it had the spirit of Champaign, with the flavour of Burgundy: and we thought it superior to either.

It appeared, however, that all our luxuries were destined, to be of short duration: on our return to Alcobaça, we found that orders had been issued to advance the following, morning.

21st.—We accordingly bid farewell to our patron, and proceeded to Batalha. This place also contains a large society of holy fathers, who, like their brethren in general, take especial care to keep up good living.—The convent here is, as I heard, so well worth seeing, than to name Batalha without making mention of it, would be quite enough to condemn a journal. I have therefore to plead for a sad deficiency; but being detained at Alcobaça. I did not arrive with the troops till so late, that seeing anything was totally out of the question; and at break of day on the——

22nd.—We marched off for Lyreia. We had good roads: they were wide, and like those of a turnpike. The town of Lyreia is very large; though the streets are narrow and bad. Its greatest ornament is the ruin of a Moorish castle constructed of height close to the walls, and commanding the country for several miles in every direction. The beauty of this ruin is completed by being surrounded with orange-groves, having the hills where it stands covered with shrubs, and its walls clothed with ivy. The castle has several partitions yet standing: among these we could plainly distinguish the remains of six separate prisons—we then took a peep at the church, which, like all others in the country, is covered with gilding and profusely ornamented. It has two organs and nine altars.

23rd.—Advanced to Pombal; where we were poorly provided for and greatly crowded. This town has also contiguous to it a fine old Moorish castle. It likewise contains a square, where there is a large market for corn, poultry, and vegetables.—The country around is supplied with small rivers; and, as you advance towards Oporto, becomes more wooded. The roads, instead of bad and broken pavement, as in the greater part of Portugal, are left like an English post-road; and are thus far more pleasant to travel upon, and not subject to be rendered nearly impassable for want of repairs, which is frequently the case in other parts of the country.

24th.—The dragoons were sent out to the neighbouring villages to make room for other troops. Our squadron took up a little hamlet called Redinha, which appeared to be the grand *depôt* for every description of vagrants and vermin.—On entering my billet (which, by the way, had a floor and a roof), I was robbed by a ragged set of people, who came a great deal too near to be pleasant; and on. my sitting down to write, those who were my fellow-lodgers stood round me, staring like savages.

The houses here, like all others in the country of inferior quality, have nothing but square holes, without glass, by way of windows: so that you have your choice of being exposed to the wind and rain, or sitting in total darkness by closing the shutters.

My berth was on the floor of a room where there were three doors that could not be kept shut, and broken boards to the light-holes. These, with a plentiful supply of chinks in the walls, rendered it as airy as being in an open field. Generally speaking, to make a remark respecting the vermin (from which scarcely a bed, from the best to the worst of houses throughout the country, is free) would be like the barber at Lisbon informing Baretti that "grapes grew in Portugal;" but here the fleas and bugs abounded to a degree worthy of memorandum. They kept me constantly employed nearly all night; and on the welcomed approach of daylight to the crevices, I sprung out of bed:—but making any havoc was of no avail:—the bugs were crawling about and the fleas swarming like ants. I therefore shuffled on my clothes, and bustled to the river; where on undressing, I found my clothes covered with fleas, and my skin spotted from head to foot. After plunging into a deep hole, and swimming round til I thought my escape from vermin tolerably complete, I put on fresh apparel, and sallied forth in search of a new billet.—After beating up the quarters of several *Senhors*, I removed my establishment to the house of a sulky old fellow, whose looks, one would think, must have kept the vermin at bay, as in his *casâ* there was not even a louse to be found.

This day (the 25th), we received orders to be in readiness to turn out for a march at the sound of the bugles. After remaining so long prepared that we were fearful some orders might have been accidentally withheld, the squadron marched on the Coimbra road, to where it led to our other quarters, and there waited for several hours, to see if the troops were coming that way

During our halt here, each man was regaled with a tumbler of good wine, brought out by the peasants, which, with many *vivas*, they presented as a testimony of their, love for the English; but when, finding the advance was countermanded, we went threes about, they put on most woeful countenances, and all appeared panic-struck. Our return to Redinha created the greatest alarm among the natives, who fancied we had been driven back by the enemy; and we being unable to explain the circumstance, kept them in a state of miserable suspense, until a Senhor Olivera, who spoke English and came to us at dinner, satisfied them with an explanation.

26th.—Instructions were issued, that, in consequence of the arrival of Sir Arthur Wellesley, the army would remain stationary till further orders.

27th.—Went out on a Portuguese sporting party—that is, with about a dozen shooters; attended by all the rabble of the village, who are armed with sticks and poles; and followed by an immense pack of dogs, consisting of every description of mongrel that can be hallooed together This procession is dosed by a *senhor* rat-catcher, who, with his bag of ferrets, brings: up the rear; and this they call hunting! I was provided with one of their best guns, which, from appearance, one would hardly know whether to prefer firing it off, or being shot at with it. Finding no other game, I mustered courage to try a shot at a few small birds, and found it killed tolerably well—Our *chasse* ended, as shooting parties usually do,—in bringing home nothing, and a set-to at eating and drinking. We had, however, no great chance of sport; as all we saw were some birds, very wild; and a rabbit, bolted by a ferret in cover.

28th.—Went to a Portuguese funeral. The corpse was laid on the back, with hands crossed, and tied together; the face quite exposed: and the body, covered with nothing, but a shroud, was carried on an open bier with a sort of tester; and thrown into a hole, like a dead dog. Instead of any solemnity at the moment of interment, the fellows around were in argumentative conversation: and one of them jumped into the grave, which was but just deep enough to bury the deceased, covered the face with a cloth, and began filling up the hole with the skulls and bones which were torn up and thrown around in digging it.

By the good management of one of our officers (who is perhaps the best forager, the choicest caterer, and the first amateur cook in his Majesty's service), we had contrived to establish an excellent mess; at which we generally went through the operation of entertaining some of the *Señors*.

On the *29th* we invited about two people to each plate, and sat down to a dinner worthy of an English host. Having just sent away the remains of the second course, we were in the very act of filling a bumper to "Sir Arthur Wellesley?" when an express arrived for us to advance immediately. The *Rouse* sounded; and in ten minutes we were all packed up and turned out. We marched to Condexa, where we did not arrive till night. This town was brilliantly illuminated, and, the flight being very dark, it appeared to advantage.—Here the left wing of the regiment halted, and we proceeded to Sarnoche.

30th.—Marched to Coimbra.—The approach of this town is one of the finest prospects in Portugal. The view of the city was the mountainous distances around, with the river Mondago winding through the richest country, is presented from an opposite height. The road then descends in a serpentine direction, leading through an olive-grove to a fine stone bridge, by which you pass into the streets of Coimbra. The buildings cover a mountain, from its very summit down to the water's edge; and the *quintas*, among the surrounding groves, extend for several miles,—This is, I believe, the largest town in Portugal, next to Lisbon and Oporto, It much resembles the former in every respect, and is equally deceiving to the traveller; who from distant appearance is led to expect a paradise, and on his entrance is disappointed with poor, narrow streets, everywhere poisoned with stink and dirt.

Our arrival was announced by a ringing of bells, which bought out crowds of the inhabitants, who lined the road, bridge, and town, to receive us with *vivas* and huzzas; and the troops, while passing, were covered with flowers from all the windows of the *Senhoras*. At night we had a grand illumination.

Coimbra is celebrated for containing the great university of the kingdom. Here, are eighteen colleges, with an extensive library; also a large convent and museum. The greater part of these are connected in a fine range of buildings, which stand on a terrace above the houses, and overlook the whole country.

May 2nd.—The greater part of the army were up, and the commander in chief arrived.

The illuminations were continued every night during our stay, and with every inducement to tempt us out; as the streets were graced with a charming supply of *Bonitas Senhoras,* who professed "*gustar muite 'os officiales Ingleses bonitos."* We were indeed, so cordially received and delightfully entertained, that it can hardly be called vanity to say we believed them in earnest.

4th.—Our regiment received orders to march out, and occupy some neighbouring villages, leaving their quarters for the 16th Dragoons; and one of our squadrons was attached (with General Tilson's brigade) to the Portuguese army.

5th.—Our division of three troops went to Brefernis; the remainder (three others) to adjacent hamlets. The roads to this place were in most parts cut through solid rocks of stone, with scarcely a crack or juncture; and their surface was ground by the cars in so many ridges, that in several parts we found it difficult to keep our horses on their legs.

Brefernis is a long league and a half from Coimbra; and, for a description of it, I couple it with Redinha, which, by the way, is far the better of the two. We took possession of the most habitable sty it afforded; and, wishing to have a reprieve from vermin as long as we could, we took our; dinner under the shade of a large tree in an orange-grove, from which we had our desert in perfection; and, I may add, with variety, as the very same tree bore two sorts of lemons, with oranges both China and Seville.[5]

In the evening we were directed; to parade, in marching order, on the following morning at four, and proceed to the sands near Coimbra, where, at six o'clock, the army was to be reviewed by the commander in chief.

---

5. Perhaps if I do not explain that the tree was grafted, this may appear a bold attempt at *Baron Munchausen.*

6th.—The regiments having formed a line (reaching above two miles), wheeled into column, marched past, and filed to their quarters.

7th.—At five in the morning with no further apprisal than the *Rouse*, we turned out; and after forming with the remainder of our brigade, proceeded forward about three leagues. The head-quarters of our regiment were at Avelans.

On the 8th we received orders to prepare for a march at five in the morning; but had to halt during that day, to afford time for Marshal Beresford, with his army, to reach the Upper Douro.

On the 9th we proceeded[6] towards the Vouga, and after having crossed the river, picqueted—as was supposed, at the distance of two leagues from the advanced posts of the enemy. On discovering this our object was, if possible, to take them by surprise; accordingly, rigid orders were issued; that during the day no man should mount a bank which touched the flank of the column, for fear of being visible to the enemy: and by night the strictest silence was preserved throughout our lines.

We marched at one on the morning of the 10th; and such extreme caution was observed in whispering the words of command, that our advanced troops moved on without being heard by those in the rear, who (being in such rocky passes, the brigade were only able to march in single file) had to form their junction under some difficulties. These were increased by the utter darkness of the night. Nor was it without danger as well as impediments, that we got forward over these rough roads, so as, by the aid of a guide, to ascertain our point. We had then arrived in a Champaign country, where our brigade advanced; on an open road, in columns of half-squadrons.

At five we came in sight of the enemy's *videttes*; formed in line; and were joined by a strong squadron of Portuguese cavalry.

---

6. In describing specifically the various movements and actions which led to the expulsion of the enemy from Oporto, particular attention would be required as to the nature of the ground, than which noise could be more disadvantageous to the operations of the cavalry.

This reconnoitre occasioned as much, surprise to the enemy, as we (by the bye) had felt on the preceding day, at hearing the French were in possession of Albergaria Nova, for which place an officer had been sent forward to procure billets for our troops.

On our skirmishers being thrown out, a kind of signal was made by the French commander, to the brigadier general who headed our party. This caused him to advance; as perhaps he judged this signal to be of a pacific nature: but he was effectually undeceived, by having three shots fired at him; when a general skirmish commenced. We soon formed to attack them in line; but finding ourselves opposed to a strong column of cavalry, we retired to a short distance.

Being then reinforced with two three-pounders from General Stuart's brigade, which immediately opened their, fire with some execution; and animated by the appearance of our infantry; we again advanced. A partial charge was made by the 16th, so as to occasion a loss to the enemy of seven men killed and a great many wounded. Of this regiment but few were wounded, and only one was taken prisoner.—We at length succeeded in driving the enemy out of the field[7]. Their retreat was to Olivera, which they soon abandoned, so as almost immediately to leave it in our possession.

The number of French cavalry here amounted to four thousand: they were supported by small detachments of infantry.—I must observe the beautiful effect of our engagement. It commenced about sunrise, in one of the finest mornings possible, on an immense tract of heath, with a pine-wood in rear of the enemy. So little was the slaughter, and regular the formations,

---

7. They were then followed by two regiments of Portuguese infantry, who drove them, in a very gallant manner, through a pine-wood, which surrounded the further end of the ground. After this they had to pass a deep and difficult ravine, which, being obliged to file, they were so long in getting through, that our artillery were there in time to play on their rear-guard, while they were scrambling up the opposite side. Their fine First Hussars came in for this: they however escaped tolerably well; they had a few killed, and their wounded were considerable; but they are so dexterous in taking them off (and behind, on their horses, if dismounted) that we are apt in general to under-calculate their numbers.

that it appeared more like a sham-fight on Wimbledon Common than an action in a foreign country.

The conduct of the Portuguese rabble was a disgrace to such a scene: they not only stripped the dead and wounded, but gave their *coup de grace* to every poor wretch who had a vital struggle remaining. The scull of one French officer in particular they broke to pieces, scattering the brains on every side. Vagabonds of this cast are observed to hover near the army during every battle.

The troops being much fatigued, and from other circumstances, halted the remainder of this day.

We were picqueted all night near Olivera; where we were at first rather in tribulation, as the batmen whom we had trusted with the *prog* had taken good care to keep out of the way. We, who were already exhausted with fagging, had to cut boughs for our huts; our fire-wood to collect, and light; and what little we could pick up, to cook for dinner. I happened to have a leveret, that in the grand scuffle had taken refuge with a poaching farrier, who popped her into his apron. My messmates then mustering a little broken bread, and adding the ribs of a dead sheep, we made out so well that we invited two friends to dine. After this we lay under our fir-boughs, and passed a very good night,

11th.—At eight in the morning we began our march; and, after advancing about two leagues, came up with the infantry, whom we found sharply engaged, driving the enemy out of a wood. A squadron of the 16th, and another of the 20th, made a charge, with the loss of several men; the road on which they acted being covered with large stones, and flanked by a wood and broad ditches. We then advanced along the main road to Oporto, which was strewed with dead men and horses, and spoils of every description. Among other objects of horror, we observed the bodies of six Portuguese hanging, besides one which had dropped down, in a state of putridity. Three of the above were suspended from a single tree. We heard that these executions took place in consequence of the murder of Soult's *aid-de-camp*; and that four of the sufferers were priests, who had refused to deliver up the real or supposed criminals.

Our pursuit of the enemy was continued for about a mile beyond Cavallos; when we were compelled to desist, in consequence of the horses being unable to bring forward the guns[8]. Near the above place the army were *bivouacqued,* with the exception of our right squadron, which remained out on picquet, attached to General Murray's brigade. We passed the night without cover; and the dews were falling so heavy as to soak our clothes and be wrung from our night-caps.

12th.—At daybreak, General Murray ordered out the picquet; and, moving on, with a subaltern and a few men, for the purpose of reconnoitring, left the remainder about a mile in advance from where we had been posted. We soon heard that the French who had engaged us were beyond the Douro, having blown up the bridge, and taken refuge in Oporto. This account being confirmed by the officer of the advanced party, orders were given that the picquet should be taken back, and wait for further instructions.

In a few hours we were informed that Sir Arthur intended passing the river that day; and our major came forward to take command of the right squadron. General Paget being in our front, with a strong division of infantry and artillery, we crossed the Douro about twelve o'clock, accompanied by General Murray's brigade, consisting of the whole Hanoverian Legion. Our passage of the river was effected about a league above Oporto: and the other brigades (in line with us to our left) crossed the river at the same time.

On landing, we took our position on a height, where we had an uninterrupted view of the town, and of the direct attack made by General Paget's division, which by this time had nearly driven the enemy from the suburbs. The remainder of the engagement consisted chiefly in skirmishing among stone walls and broken rocks, with which the country is much intersected.—We could

---

8. At this I am not surprised, being informed, by an officer of artillery, that, out of three hundred horses sent for their service, from Portsmouth, there arrived at Lisbon only eighty that could be called effective.

see for several miles in every direction, and distinctly observe the whole of the enemy's cavalry retreating. Orders were then given to make an attempt to cut off some of the rear troops; but these orders were recalled before the squadron had proceeded a quarter of a mile, as the general soon perceived that the enemy's covering party was too strong for us.

After rejoining the German Legion battalions on the height, we descended to the valley, making a flank movement for some distance parallel to the Douro, with a view of advancing as a reserve in the rear of those engaged.—While General Murray was making a momentary reconnoitre, a staff-officer came up, with the information that one of our regiments was very hard pressed, and that the cavalry must advance immediately for its support. On this, we hastened forward as fast as was possible from the nature of the ground; and, after surmounting many impediments among the stone walls got into the main road, on reaching the outskirts of the town.—Our infantry here extended along the road. We then, forming up in threes, passed all our lines at a full gallop; whilst they greeted us with one continued huzza.

After this, going almost at speed, enveloped in a cloud of dust, for nearly two miles, we cleared our infantry, and that of the French appeared. A strong body was drawn up in close column. With bayonets ready to receive us in front. On each flank of the road was a stone wall, bordered outwardly by trees; with other walls, projecting in various directions; so as to give every advantage to the operations of infantry, and to screen those by whom we were annoyed. On our left, in particular, numbers were posted in a line, with their pieces rested on the wall which flanked the road, ready to give us a running fire as we passed. This could not but be effectual, as our left men by threes were nearly close to the muzzles of the muskets, and barely out of the reach of a *coup de sabre*. In a few seconds, the ground was covered with men and horses: notwithstanding these obstacles, we penetrated the battalion opposed to us; the men of which, relying on their bayonets, did not give way till we were nearly close upon it, when they fled in great confusion. For some time this contest was kept up, hand to hand; and, for the time it lasted, was severe.

After many efforts, we succeeded in cutting off three hundred, most of whom were secured as prisoners: but our own loss was very considerable. Our squadron consisted of scarcely forty file; and the brunt of the action, of course, fell the heaviest on the troop in front: of the fifty-two men composing it, ten were killed, eleven severely wounded (besides others slightly), and six taken prisoners: of the four officers engaged, three were on the wounded list. For my own part; my horse being shot under me, the moment after a ball had grazed my upper lip, I had to scramble my way on foot, amidst the killed and wounded—among whom the enemy, from the side walls, were continually firing—and thus effected my escape from this agreeable situation. On the approach of our infantry, the French brigade was compelled to retire Our few remaining men, coming threes about, brought with them the prisoners in triumph.

Our commanding officer and squadron had the satisfaction of receiving thanks from the commander in chief. On the merits of our charge, the comment of the French general ought not to be omitted: he sent for our men (who had been his prisoners, and afterwards escaped), and declared to them, that, in his opinion, "we must have all been drunk, or mad; as the brigade we had attacked was nearly two thousand strong[9]."

The town of Oporto, to which we retired[10], exhibited a scene of the greatest confusion: the streets were strewed with dead horses and men, and the gutters dyed with blood.—This night the town was illuminated, in honour of our success. The effect, however, could not be very brilliant, as the late exactions of the

---

9. On returning, we met our second squadron, about a mile to the rear, which had just passed the river and was hastening to our support, though too late: our third was still on the other side the water; and our fourth being detached, we had only one squadron that came into the above action. Two were mentioned in the *Dispatches*.

10. Scarcely any farther engagement took place that evening: it was then about five o'clock; and our infantry, taking the advance, remained near the position where our charge was made, being about three miles from the town.

French had left the poor inhabitants in a state to testify their joy more by good-will than deed.

We were all night, and half the next day, employed in seeking our wounded, who had been taken into different houses on the road.

So wholly unexpected was our forcing the passage of the Douro on the 12th that the French were totally unprepared for us, and Marshal Soult was roused from his dinner to put his plans, of defence in execution: but of how little avail was this defence, and to how short a time protracted!—In his precipitate retreat, the enemy abandoned a large proportion of artillery, with ordnance stores, ammunition, and baggage.

It is but due, to ascribe the brilliant successes of this day, not only to the determined bravery of British troops, but also to the experienced judgement of the commander in chief, and the rapidity of his movements.

13th.—The army continued to advance, the infantry being in front. We remained in Oporto to collect and make arrangements for our wounded. What with the number of men left sick by the enemy, and those taken in since the action, the hospitals were completely filled.—This day the dead were buried, and the streets cleared.—We went to see the remains of the bridge that had been destroyed: it having only consisted of a chain of boats we were ill repaid for the difficulty in finding out way through the intricate part of the town which led to it.—Oporto was much deserted by the inhabitants, and had a dismal appearance: some of the best mansions were left well furnished, with closets full of costly china, and almost every household utensil still remaining.

This city being too well known to require the concise description that would fall to its share in a pocket-book. I only observe, that, from its choice buildings and eminent situation, it surpassed, in my estimation, all the towns yet seen in Portugal.

14th.—Our regiment assembled at two in the afternoon, and about three marched for Villa Nova. Fifty campaigns may not produce greater miseries than we had to encounter before we reached this place. We started on a very bad road, in a wet evening; and, by the time we were soaked to the skin, it became so dark, that we could not see our way; of which the guide himself had but an imperfect knowledge, even by daylight. After crawling on till the horses were knocked up, and the men scarcely able to keep their eyes open, we were cheered with some lights, which indicated our approach to a village. We all thanked our stars that we had at last found the quarters.

We had soon, however, the consolation to find that we had wandered to the wrong place, and were quite out of our path to Villa Nova. We had then to wait while another guide was pressed; and the hamlet we were in was so crowded with infantry, that not one of us could get under an empty shed. After sitting, benumbed with cold, for hear an hour, we proceeded with our new conductor, who was a lame fellow—consequently a very slow goer. In a piteous tone he declared it would be morning before we could reach Villa Nova, and that he was himself doubtful of being able to find the road. It was so dark we were forced to be every moment halloing to each other, to avoid being lost; and the men so repeatedly mistook the road, that we had often to stop and sound the bugle, for, half an hour at a time, before we could get them together.

We were the whole night without the least shelter, in an incessant pour of rain, scrambling with our horses among the rocks, expecting every moment to be thrown down; and, in places where the safety of our lives required dismounting, we had to wade through deep streams of water, occasioned by the torrents of rain which flooded the passes. We were latterly every now and then dropping asleep on our horses, quite exhausted, and shivering the whole time with, cold. After suffering every hardship that could attend upon a mere march, we reached Villa Nova; where we had to remain an hour in the streets; the rain still continuing.—At last, some sheds were provided, and we filed off. It was then past six o'clock, which extended the duration of our drenching to sixteen hours. Our servants were lost;

so that we had neither meat, drink nor clothing. I got into a stable, where, on some dirty straw, I slept, in my wet clothes, till two o'clock in the afternoon.

15th.—The chief part of the army, which had been here, went forward; we were unable to proceed that day,

16th.—Advanced to Braga. We halted to receive forage and rations, and then proceeded to Gregio Novo. The weather was wet, the troops miserably accommodated, and the officers were all bundled into a hovel like a drove of pigs. The infantry were kept on the advance,—No engagement of any consequence, had taken place; and the French continued their retreat.

Previously to our reaching Gregio Novo, the advanced posts sent in about fifty prisoners, who were all kennelled in a church; in the middle of which they had made a comfortable fire with the gilded wood that had decorated the altars.

17th.—Marched to Salamundé, where we passed the army, and went in advance, accompanied by the Guards, who had the preceding evening been skirmishing with some success; for the enemy, finding themselves hard pressed, were constantly throwing away their knapsacks, which they had so loaded with plunder as to be unable to march with them. Everyone, therefore, who could lay hands on a Frenchman or his kit, had a fine prize. These marauders had robbed the churches of pieces of gold and silver, which, when we entered Salamundé, we were told our soldiers had taken and melted down. A number of silver forks, spoons, &c., were sold here by regular auction. Some of the most valuable stones were bought at a tenth part of what they were worth; and the men would rather receive the most trifling sums for their prizes, than be at the trouble of carrying them.

The village of Salamundé was a perfect scene of devastation; and on every road around the French had set fire to the cottages of the peasants: several of these were in flames as we passed. Dead men, horses, cattle, and everything that could forcibly depict ruin, were here again strewed for leagues along the road. They had a number of horses and mules, which they deemed it expedient to leave; and in order to render them totally unserviceable, cut the sinews of their hind legs, and left a field full of these hamstrung animals.[11]

As we were this day not up with the enemy, no affairs of out-posts took place. The Guards kept in front, and our regiment occupied two straggling hamlets to the right. On taking up our quarters (which, like the other houses in this part of the country, were little cabins of loose stones), we found that the few wretched inhabitants who had been left, taking us for their former visitors, had precipitately fled to the mountains. In the billet I occupied, they had very kindly left me a large fire, with a pot of soup boiling on it—It had rained day and night, incessantly, till this evening: the clouds then began to break, and gave us a grand view of the setting sun behind the mountains.

18th.—Marched to Monta Legre, a small town on the frontiers, to the left of Chaves, which was our last advance. The pursuit of the enemy was relinquished by reason of Marshal Beresford's army being unable, through extreme fatigue, to proceed farther than Chaves; and consequently not being forward enough to cut off their retreat, as was intended.

The French, however, found themselves so hard pressed, they were forced to abandon nearly all their artillery, and, in short, every encumbrance, to facilitate their escape. This forced march rendered their loss, both in men and horses, very considerable: but Mr. Soult had taken good care to secure his plunder, by sending the train of carts that were loaded with it, well to the rear; and having them always dispatched a day or two before his troops.

Monta Legre had been so despoiled, that the natives were nearly famished, and we had to trust entirely to the arrival of our own short stock of provisions. Nothing could be found here in the way either of meat, drink, or vegetables; save a few starved goats, bad water, and dead cabbage-stalks.

---

11. This barbarous custom is frequently resorted to by a retreating army, when ammunition cannot be spared to shoot them.

19th.—The whole army halted.

Being on the borders of Spain, I was desirous of seeing this country, and set out for that purpose; but had to pay handsomely for indulging my curiosity.

After passing a country strewed with French, who had been left to die by sickness and famine, I reached the Village of Padreira; which had been stripped of everything, left in flames, and its inhabitants (nearly naked) in a state of starvation.—Having mounted the hills, a fog came on, and I was lost. Here, without either sword, pistol, or stick, several Portuguese met me, who, I am convinced, suspected me to be a Frenchman: and a constant example was before my eyes of what would be my fate, had they decided on this mistake; for, in every direction, lay the corpses of stragglers and helpless men whom they had murdered.

Though the fog was mended by a heavy rain, I was determined to proceed; being told I was within half a league of Spain. The passes were among low woods on the declivity of mountains; and so bad, that even at a foot-pace they were nearly impassable. The *Senhor's* half league proved about six English miles; and just as I reached the borders of Gallicia, my horse was taken with the staggers, and for a long time unable to move. It was then growing dusk, the rain pouring, and I, ten miles from my quarters. My mind was decided that neither the old horse nor his master would see England again: and indeed the chance was greatly against us; but, most fortunately, General Sylveira's Portuguese army came by in about half an hour after, and, to crown all, was bound for Monta Legre. With these troops I marched, halfway up to my knees in mud, leading, or rather hauling along, my Rosinante; which there was so much difficulty in doing, that the column was all the time gaining ground of me. Several times I expected to be left behind, lost, and (what would of course follow to a stranger here at night) put to death; and repeatedly observed the blood-thirsty looks of the savages composing this army, who, so far as I could understand, were holding forth on their suspicions of me. I heard one of them say, "I believe that fellow to be no friend of ours."—It soon became quite dark;

and, after having gone about seven miles, my horse dropped dead. I then took my appointments on my back, and could keep up with the best of them; and about eleven, at night we reached our destination.

20th.—Our regiment returned to Salamundé by a different route from that by which we had advanced. The road here winds round the great mountains, adhering to immense precipices; and is in many places so narrow, as barely to admit a mule with baggage. You are nearly the whole day in a chain of mountains, among woods, rocks, and water-falls: the distances that catch the eye between the heights, opposed to this varied fore-ground, present a charming landscape. Everything has the most wild and romantic appearance; and, amidst the awful roar of surrounding cascades, you may conceive yourself deserted by every earthly creature.

The passes, as everywhere else, were strewed with dead men; the majority of whom were in the most offensive state of putridity. The French had so many horses precipitated down the heights, that we concluded they must have passed them in the dark. We saw several lying at the bottom, apparently quite mangled by the fall.

22nd,—Marched to Botica, where we dined and slept in the gallery of a little chapel, left, like everything elsewhere the French had been, in a state of ruin.

23rd.—Proceeded to Braga; leaving, on our left, a castle and other buildings curiously constructed on an immense solid rock. We passed also a valley which contained a great number of huge stones, several of which were forty yards in girth,—We were to halt at Braga till further orders.

Braga, the capital of Entre Minho e Douro, contains many good houses, with broad and commodious streets. This town is well supplied with most of the articles which the country affords. Here are a number of good shops, an excellent market, and mechanics for almost every kind of work.

On the *28th* we went to the mass at the, cathedral. In this church there is a gallery, called the Bishop's Chapel, with some of the best carving we had seen. Here are three organs; one in the English style, about the middle of the aisle; and two others, with horizontal pipes, which stand on each side the gallery; to one of these there is a curious figure, which marks time for the music by means of a spring to its hand. The decorations of this church are so nearly in the style of those in the church of Alcobaça, that it would be needless here to give any description; and as for valuables——the French had been there!

31st—Marched to Villa Nova.

June 1st.—Re-entered Oporto, where we halted till the 3rd. The regiment then left this town, and passed the Douro over a temporary bridge of boats. Here we saw the richest vineyards for several miles down the banks of the river; and the city of Oporto, being built on the declivity of a mountain, appeared to the greatest advantage from the opposite side.—We then marched three leagues on an execrable road, and came to a village called Gregio, By continuing parallel to the sea, we had it in view nearly all day. Between the beach and the above place there is a very large convent, with extensive gardens, and several fine fountains.

From Gregio there is nothing for a journal, unless I state that seven of us had to inhabit a hovel that would scarcely hold a pair, of bullocks, and where, within a slight partition, there was an old woman dying.—This evening the wet weather again returned; and on the 4th, after all getting well ducked, we reached Olivera. The rain compelling us to told our heads constantly down, we had a fine opportunity of inspecting the variety of marble which composed a part of the road leading to the above place.

5th.—We proceeded to Agueda. On my road to this place I experienced the comforts of being taken ill on service. My complaint proceeding from a violent cold, our regimental Æsculapians ordered me, on my arrival in quarters, to "go to bed" to, "keep quiet, and promote perspiration!!!"—I had a nice opportunity of following this prescription! After shaking like a man with the ague, and waiting for half an hour, a Portuguese bed (that is, a hard straw bag on hard boards) was provided, with dirty blankets and damp sheets. My room had a thorough draught of air, and the rain kept pouring in. The savages of the billet refused me a little fire-wood; and had not my satellites made a proper use of their feet, as well as their hands, I could not have got my broth boiled.—The situation here was as well calculated for "keeping quiet" as the ringing of bells, crying of children, barking of curs, and squalling of cats, would admit of. The Portuguese were all day running about the house in their wooden shoes; their tongues, as well as their feet, being in perpetual motion.

6th.—I was alive, and went through the rain to Alamera, where the troops had arrived. They halted here till the 8th, and then went to Coimbra.—On our return to this town, a great part of the regiment was sent over the bridge. The officers of our squadron were in high luck at the distribution of billets: we were quartered in the house of a nobleman, which was left in care of his son, a colonel in the Portuguese service. Here we received the kindest attention, and, having every comfort we could require, established a sumptuous mess; for which, we had an abundance of plate and the best services of china,

This house is very large, with an extensive suite of rooms; and has a lawn before it, with a view of the river and town. We had excellent stabling, and a field to turn out our horses.—Behind the premises there are a fine garden and orange-grove. At the farther end, among the most solitary shades is a large fountain: hence arose the name of this q*uinta,—Casâ da Lacryma (the Home of Tears);* and which is derived from the following melancholy circumstance:—

Alphonso IV. King of Portugal, having married his son to a Spanish Princess, took this seat, as a villa for the young couple. On coming here to reside they brought their bride-maid, a most beautiful young Spanish lady, to whom the Prince himself evinced. a great partiality. The Princess died a few years after; and he became so enamoured of this Donna, that he made her his wife.

On the King hearing of this match, and having provided another, in his opinion far more advantageous, in the moment of his rage he sent two Spanish counsellors to murder the beloved bride of his son. The villains accomplished their horrid act one evening, when she was walking by this fountain. The distracted state of his son's mind, together with the stings of his own conscience, soon brought Alphonso to his grave; and on the Prince ascending the throne, the assassins were executed; the body of his late wife was dug up; the crown of Portugal placed on her head; and she conveyed in state to Alcobaça, where she was re-interred with every tribute of honour and affection,

13th, 14th, and 15th.—We marched to Condexa, Pombal, and Lyreia. This evening we spent agreeably, at the house of a *Don Senhor,* whose lady sent orders to the steward of her *quinta* to provide for our reception the succeeding day.

On the 16th we took up our abode there, and fared luxuriously.

The regiment occupied two small towns—Aldea de Cruz, and Orense. These places are in a wooded and rich country: the latter has a fine Moorish castle.

We had this day turned off to the left of the great Lisbon road, on our way to Thomar, where we arrived on the 17th; the head-quarters of the army being then established at Abrantes.

At Thomar we came up with the 1st German Hussars, who marched out soon after our arrival. The army were also reinforced by the 23rd Dragoons, and a heavy brigade;—all landed while we were up the country. The four troops of the 20th had left us, to join the remainder of that regiment in Sicily; and our force of cavalry was then six regiments.

Thomar is a fine old Moorish town, prettily situated on the banks of the Naboan, and commanded by an immense height, on which there remains one of the finest castles in Portugal. Contiguous to this stands a large convent, which, excepting one troop, contained our whole regiment: we had there about five hundred horses.

22nd.—Walked up the river, shaded by orchards, where the trees were breaking down with fruit, and everything around had the richest appearance. While we were in silent admiration contemplating the beauties of nature, a volley of dirt-clods was pelted at us by some Portuguese. What we had done to offend them I know not; but suppose, judging by themselves, they thought us thieves, and concluded we were planning operations to attack their orchard. Justice herself directed us to give them chase; and, after soundly thrashing those who were not then in wind for running away, we proceeded up the river.

Above two miles from the town we came to an artificial water-fall, which filled the whole valley with its echo. Being intercepted by a rising ground, it bursts suddenly upon the view with a majestic appearance. The stream flows over two flights of steps, regularly built with stone, and forming an obtuse angle in the centre. The fall is near sixty feet, and extends about a hundred yards.—This immense torrent of water is carried off in a winding stream, which, by an increased rapidity when recovered from the force of the cascade, is evidently the whole way on a descent.

During our stay at Thomar, we were civilly treated, and often entertained with musical parties. At these we were sometimes enchanted, by a pot-bellied fellow, who was allowed to be the first guitar-player in the kingdom. Paltry as the powers of this instrument may appear, we thought that in his hands it produced one of the finest solos we had ever heard.

July 1st.—Received orders to proceed on the advance for Spain,

2nd.—Marched off at four o'clock in the morning; and in the afternoon reached Villa de Rea, where we *bivouacqued.*— This day the mules and *calèche* of our commanding officer had an extraordinary escape. The vehicle, which was loaded with valuable baggage, china, glass, &c, was overturned, and hurled down a precipice for twenty yards. At the bottom of this is a river, from which all was saved by lodging among the rocks. Instead (as we expected) of seeing everything dashed to pieces, and the mules killed, all we found amiss was, the breaking of the splinter bar and two bottles. By the greatest accident, there happened to be no one in the carriage; and the driver scrambled off when he found his mules giving way.

4th.—Marched for Cortesada, where (after passing a deserted town, and a perfect amphitheatre of mountains) we arrived and picqueted.—Here we had nine horses starved to death, and many others were in a most deplorable condition.

5th.—Proceeded to Larzidas, a large village, so forsaken by its inhabitants that every house was empty but about three or few, in which there remained the families of a few miserable peasants.—The bullocks[12] not coming up till late in the evening, we were, as usual, in a bad way for provision; and at this place even water was so scarce that we were forced to put a sentry over what could be discovered, and which was very bad.

6th.—Continued to advance, and picqueted near Castello Branco; where we were reinforced by our fourth squadron, which had arrived from General Beresford's army, then left in the north.

This day we passed, on our left, the Estrella (or Star) mountain, the highest in Portugal; on which we could plainly distinguish the snow, though supposed to be nine leagues from the road.

Our route specified that we were to halt at Castello Branco; but on our arrival we found that it was countermanded; and, in our exhausted state, advanced, on the 7th, to Lodoeiro—The officers were here in little cabins; and about eleven at night a fire broke out, which consumed a great part of them. The inhabitants of, this hamlet were in such a state of apathy they never at-

---

12. It is common, when we come to a camp touch, to have our half-starved bullocks up, down, and in the pot, the same day.

tempted to assist, nor even save their own property, till their very houses were caught by the flames.

8th.—Marched to a wood near Lodoeiro—The country we had passed appeared to abound with a variety of birds. The eagles and vultures were constantly hovering over the rear of the troops, and several times came within fair shot.—There is also a small species of land tortoise, one of which our men caught in a shed.

9th.—Proceeded on our march.—This being a clear day, we were presented with the grand mountains in our front, and, while so intensely hot we could scarcely breathe, we plainly saw the snow with which several of their summits were covered.— After advancing three leagues, we crossed the river Elga, which in that part divides the two kingdoms, and (leaving Salvateira, and a Moorish castle, to our right) entered Spain. The inhabitants of the two countries seem to have no communication, with, or knowledge of each other. We surveyed the town of Zarza Mayor, which appeared very little different from those we had seen in Portugal: the Spanish, however, in their houses, seem neater and cleaner than the Portuguese.

This day the regiment came up with the remainder of the brigade, and *bivouacqued* three miles from Zarza Mayor—In the evening we had to pitch our boughs in a forest, where we were tortured the whole night by gnats, and annoyed with every description of reptile, and by a concert of toads and frogs, which were by no means unlike Portuguese women in a market.—In the morning, my face was swelled with bites; and the blankets between which I laid would have been a treat to no one but Sir J—— B——.

Nothing could well exceed the variety of insects, with which these blankets would have furnished the amateur: he might have obtained the finest specimens of the beetle—the choicest old spiders—and swarms of ants, which in these warm countries are half an inch in length.

After getting up, I bathed in some water near; and, while dressing on the bank, there were around me enough of the large

Spanish lizards to supply half the museums in London.—I was afterwards congratulated on neither being sucked by a leech nor bit by a water-snake, both of which are said to abound in this water.

11th.—After halting the 10th, we renewed our march at four o'clock a. m.; and in the evening got to a wood, a short half-league from Morealega.

12th.—We entered Coria; whence we were sent half a league put of our line of march, and picqueted at least a mile from any water. The wood we were in contained a variety of the most curious Spanish birds, with which the trees were full everywhere round the camp.—This country, and I believe almost every other in Spain, abounds with game: some of the German Legion, who had brought their guns with them, were out only a few hours, and came home loaded with red-legged partridges.

I rode to Coria, a large town, on a vast eminence. Here is a fine church, through which I was shown by a priest. It has towers, with parapets overlooking the whole country. Its inside, as well as its ornaments, differs little of nothing from the churches in Portugal. An organ it has on so large a scale, that the bellows are blown by means of two boys running hand in hand up and down a see-saw of flat timber.

The holy father told me, that this was the finest instrument in Spain, and that the pipes were all pure silver. For the latter I have only his word; but the organ spoke for itself: I never heard any, thing to equal its tone; and the different stops produced a chaste and tasteful imitation of every instrument.—In the town of Coria we had iced lemonade, frozen with the snow brought, above nine, leagues, from the mountain tops.

13th.—Marched; crossed the river Alagon; and picqueted near Galisteia, a town with intricate streets, on a strong position, and fortified by a Moorish wall.

14th.—This day we passed through a country full of game:— an officer, and, myself, by merely flanking the regiment the march, with one old gun between us, killed a fine bag of Spanish partridges and wild-pigeons.—About midday we entered Placentia, a large town on the Xera, where, the army had assembled. We had excellent ground for camp, close to the town: the lines of our brigade were on a green as level as a billiard-table, shaded by large trees; and by making our huts on the banks of the river, we had only to take a swim and lie down again, whenever, we felt it too hot.

17th.—Received orders to advance the next day.

On the *18th* we marched about five leagues, and *bivouacqued* in the forest on the banks of the Tieter.

19th.—Continued to advance through the forest; and, after a fatiguing march of eight leagues, halted for the night near the river. Our position was sheltered by a range of mountains covered with snow, which appeared as if close to us, though at the distance of about twelve miles. The day being clear, we had a distinct view of their summits, the height of which is so immense, that we perceived a few small clouds hanging near them in the sky, without reaching above one third of their stupendous elevation.

After pursuing our march for some time; on the 20th we got clear of the forest, and passed a plain of above three leagues in extent; the dry sand of which strongly reflected the intense heat of the day, without affording us the shelter of a single tree.

Leaving the town of Oropeza to our left, we picqueted for the night near Lugo-Terra, situated on the same chain of hills. A large pomegranate-tree here saved some of us the trouble of building a hut, and thus made amends for the late barrenness of the sultry plain.—We here received information that five hundred French cavalry, sent on a foraging party, had quitted Lugo-Terra, on the day before our arrival.—General Anson's brigade, with four regiments of infantry, were on the advance.

On the 21st we were passed by the whole of the Spanish army, amounting to at least forty-two thousand. Their infantry, in part only, had a good appearance: but many of their cavalry were in a ragged state, without boots, and some of them literally with bare feet. Their horses, though slight, were in other respects good; yet with bad appointments, ill put on insomuch, that their stirrups were so long as hardly to be reached with the toe pointed down.

We remained saddled, ready to turn out on the shortest notice.—In the evening we marched on. Having passed Oropeza, the whole British army was drawn up, for General Cuesta's inspection, and afterwards picqueted in the contiguous fields. Our station was close to a small village, through which we had passed.

We came up with the Spanish troops on the 22nd, whom we found engaged in a skirmish on an immense plain. Our army soon supported them in great force, advancing in readiness to give the enemy battle; but they continued to retreat through Talavera, which they evacuated, with the loss of a few men; and fell back to a strong position above a league from it, on the other side of the Tagus. We remained *bivouacqued* between Talavera and the Alberche, in readiness to advance.

This was a fagging day for the troops; for, after being up nearly all the preceding night, we had begun our march: at four in the morning; and it was near seven in the evening when we had halted. An hour then elapsed before any provision could be got; and that some of us had to leave to go on picquet, which kept us on the alert all night.—In the interim, we heard that our cavalry in advance near the Alberche (the 23rd Dragoons and 1st Hussars of the King's German Legion) had been fired on from a masked battery, near to which they advanced to attack a small body of the enemy, drawn up as if with an intention of resisting.

This brigade lost ten horses; but, fortunately, no men were killed. And, we were told, that about the same time Sir Arthur had a narrow escape while reconnoitring; having been fired at with a three-pound shot, which cut a bough from a tree close to his head.

On the 23rd we received orders to march at five; but these were countermanded, and our advance was postponed till the following day; in consequence, as we were afterwards told, of General Cuesta's unwillingness to go forward—for various reasons—all beyond the comprehension of those, to whom the immediate attack promised every success.

In the evening we heard that the French had occupied a very strong position (according to report, with entrenchments) about a league and a half from the town; and that their army, calculated at nearly thirty thousand, was to be reinforced by twelve thousand more. We had not the smallest doubt but a very severe action would take place, as it was the known determination of Sir Arthur to attack them early the following morning.

24th.—After hearing the road in one continued rattle all night, with the marching of artillery, we turned out at two a.m. With the infantry in advance, we moved on, till the approach of day. The cavalry then halted, and dismounted, while the front of the British column, which extended considerably above a league, was fording the river to the left; and the Spaniards, on the right, passing the bridge, under the heights.

We expected every moment to hear a tremendous cannonading; till, after waiting some time, uncertain what could occasion the delay of the attack, we received information that the French had retreated during the night. In consequence of this, our orders were to return to the environs of Talavera, and there to remain picqueted till further instructions. The Spanish army was in advance.

Talavera is a large town, with rather intricate streets, and was formerly celebrated for its silk-manufactory. Most of the inhabitants have been driven out by the late excesses of the French. Close to our camp were the ruins of a most extensive and beautiful amphitheatre: the rotunda appeared to have been occupied by cavalry. Here also the remains of a large church are added to the general marks of dilapidation.

On the *25th* and *26th* we remained encamped round Talavera, destitute of almost every article of provision. On the latter day, the advanced guard of General Cuesta was driven from its position near Torrijos, when his army retired to the right bank of the Alberche. After this, all the movements of the enemy indicated the design of a general action.

At one in the morning of the, 27th, the cavalry were ordered to make a patrol. We marched in the dark; and at daybreak arrived at the bank of the river Alberche, opposite the spot where the French had been lately encamped. We then halted, waiting for further orders, and hearing various reports:—some, asserted that our picquets were driven in by the enemy; others, that the Spanish troops in front, with General Mackenzie's division, were engaged: but the prevailing opinion was, that the French had entirely retreated, and that we should see no more of them till we got near Madrid.

After a suspense of about three hours, we received orders to advance, and cross the river. Before we had marched a league, we met all the baggage of the advanced posts on the return, and the infantry retreating. The division thus pressed was that of General Mackenzie, which was attacked by a greatly superior force while falling back on the main body of the army.—General Mackenzie was posted near the wood on the right of the Alberche, with a division of infantry and a brigade of cavalry.

Of our combined force, the Spaniards formed the right wing, in front of Talavera; the ground before them (from which they took care not to advance) being covered with olive-groves, and much intersected by ditches. The open ground to the left was the station of the British: as this was commanded by a height, Major-General Hill's division was posted there, in a second line, and had to maintain the positopn against repeated attacks of the enemy.—Another position, in the centre of the two armies, was secured by our brigade of dragoons and some Spanish cavalry.

The enemy's force, which more than twice exceeded ours, was composed of the united corps of Marshal Victor and General Sebastian, besides nearly eight thousand of Joseph Buonaparte's Guards, and the garrison of Madrid.

But, reverting to our first advance. With the Spanish cavalry on our right, we formed on a large plain; where the enemy advanced on us in such a strength that we were driven back to Talavera; their *videttes* maintaining a skirmish with ours till within a mile of the town.—We went into camp, but received immediate orders to turn out again, the whole army being under arms, for the support of General Mackenzie's division, which, with a brigade of six six-pounders, had hitherto sustained the efforts of the enemy.—For this purpose the cavalry re-advanced.

We had no sooner reached the plain, than we found ourselves under a heavy cannonade, particularly on the left, from the range of hills, near a wood. We then fell back on the heights to the left of Talavera.

In the dusk of the evening the enemy began a very warm action with the artillery and infantry, the latter of whom were engaged nearly all night; and a little before dark the enemy made an attempt, with Polish cavalry, to break through the Spanish lines, and enter Talavera. On this the Spaniards opened a fire from right to left, by which these Poles were put to flight.—Our cavalry were then in the rear.

Formed in open column, we laid down, with our horses' bridles round our arms, till midnight, when we were roused by a sharp firing on the left. This was occasioned by an attempt of the enemy to gain possession of the height occupied by the division of General Hill. After an obstinate struggle, and a momentary appearance of success, they were repulsed in a very spirited manner by the bayonet.

Whole battalions of the enemy had got into our line; some calling out that they were "Spanish;" and others, that they were "Germans deserting:" our old soldiers, however, soon discovered their "*ruse de guerre*," and gave them enough of coming to close quarters.

28th.—About two o'clock in the morning our attention was again called to a very heavy firing from the wood in front of Talavera. The Spaniards, as we afterwards learnt, had opened their fire on their own *videttes*, whom, from the darkness of the night, they had mistaken for the enemy. Similar mistakes occurred throughout the armies.

During the night-engagements, our battalions, as well as those of the enemy, fought with such determined fury, as frequently to close in, and beat out each other's, brains with their muskets. At half past five a. m. the attack was renewed on General Hill's position, and was again repelled with distinguished bravery—The two armies then continued sharply engaged till about eleven o'clock, when the attack of the French was suspended. They then rested their troops; and, we heard, cooked their dinners in the field of battle.—We were at the same time cheered with the welcome appearance of some wine, which, with a little bread, was issued to our troops,

About noon the engagement was renewed, and became general; when the firing of musketry was heard, on all sides, like the roll of a drum, with scarcely a moment's intermission, accompanied by a heavy cannonade; and thus continued during the remainder of the day.—Our infantry could not but suffer most severely during such a general slaughter: several regiments, on both sides, were nearly cut to pieces, many companies being reduced from seventy-five to nine or ten men.—The dragoons on the right did not come forward till the afternoon, when they were called on to support General Sherbrooke's division.

After making our way through a grove of olives in some confusion, we gained the open ground, and had to form under an incessant fire, of artillery and musketry; the small shot literally pouring in like a shower of hail.—On the left, of the line were the 23rd Dragoons and 1st German Hussars, who advanced against some French columns, which were marching on General Hill's division by way of the valley. This brigade was ordered to charge; but the enemy, having soon formed in two solid squares, were too well prepared for their reception; and, to increase the disadvantages under which this attack was made, there was, between these regiments and the enemy, a large ditch. Notwithstanding the confusion this occasioned, the 23rd Dragoons persevered in the charge; and, though with a most serious loss, penetrated the French battalions.[13]

I here assert, that several of the Spanish Cavalry ran away: some of whom were seen robbing the poor women belonging to the British army, whom they found on the road, crying, and anxiously alarmed for the fate of their husbands. One poor wretch (of our regiment) they not only plundered of everything in her possession, but took her very clothes, and an ass, on which, from her infirmity she was obliged to travel. The cruelty practised by some of our allies exceeded everything that can be conceived. I was informed—and I believe it—that; after robbing, stripping, and putting to death, several of our wounded, a party of them had the impudence to appear before our officers, relating their own enormities, with seeming horror, and imputing them to the French. Their guilt appeared manifest, however, from the appointments of the unfortunate sufferers being found in their possession.—Added to this, so completely did the Spaniards in general monopolise every article of provision, that, to the period above described, many of us had been nearly three days without receiving bread, or any kind of sustenance. This may in some measure, perhaps, be attributed to a want of exertion in many of our commissariat.

To return from this digression.—The battle raged, with equal obstinacy on both sides, till the close of day; when, after a most sanguinary contest, the action ceased; each party maintaining the same position.—During the night the enemy retreated, and crossed the river Alberche in perfect order; leaving us in possession of the field of battle.

Thus the hard-fought action was decidedly gained by the matchless bravery of British troops. Nothing could exceed the valour of our infantry and cavalry during the whole of the above engagements; and our artillery was also highly conspicuous, though labouring under the disadvantage of having no horses in reserve.—The effect of Colonel Sharpnell's shells was fatally ruinous to the enemy's columns, which by these were frequently

---

13. The ground where this attack was made &c. will be seen in the plan (frontispiece).

broken: but it was lamentable, during the day, to see the fuses set fire to the grass, by which many of the wounded were burnt.— We had thirty pieces of artillery—*viz*. nineteen six-pounders, five five-and-half inch howitzers, and six three-pounders. The French had upwards of sixty pieces of cannon, most of which were eight-pounders: and, it must be observed, they were so directed towards the British, that scarcely a shot was fired at the Spaniards during the whole of the 28th.

In taking further notice of our allies, I much wish that what I have to say of them was at all in their praise. Their numbers amounted to between thirty and forty thousand effective in the field. During the whole of the attack on the 28th (directed entirely against the British line), they remained almost wholly inactive[14]—except a great number of them whom I, and indeed most of the British officers, saw running away.—Throughout the engagement, numbers of the Spaniards were constantly disappearing.

We heard of two regiments, in particular, who ran away on the evening of the 27th, frightened by the firing of their own troops on the right; and the posts from which they deserted were occupied, by command of Sir Arthur, with troops from the second line.—Piles of Spanish arms were left loaded in the field.

From what I am going to add, it may be ascertained, that the inhabitants of Talavera possessed as little humanity, as the generality of the heroes had shown disposition for the combat, whilst posted to our right, for its nominal defence.—About an hour before the close of the last engagement, it was my chance to receive a wound: in consequence, I was carried to Talavera; and, on my arrival, the Spaniards refused to let me come within their thresholds.

Thus was I left, bleeding, in the street; surrounded by the

---

14. Feeling myself bound, as well as fully disposed, to make mention of what exceptions I saw, or even heard of, I have to name two Spanish battalions, under General Whittingham, who came forward to support the Guards; some squadrons of cavalry on our left; with General Bassecourt's division, and part of their artillery.

most pitiable and horrid objects that can be imagined, who were lying on the pavement, screaming and groaning, without the soothing of compassion or succour of any kind.—At length I proved more fortunate than my fellow-sufferers, through the kind assistance of an officer, who, being on hospital guard, had a billet, and gave me up his bed—which (we having for nineteen previous nights slept in the fields, and generally without shelter) was rendered a novelty. Here I remained, reflecting, during a sleepless night, on the many who had to endure far worse than myself.

My case, in being refused admission at Talavera, was by no means a singular one. An officer, who had a billet there, which he had occupied some time, was brought back to it in a predicament similar to my own: like myself, he was refused the shelter of a roof, and left fainting in the streets, till some soldiers forced open the door.

After the battle, we heard that the French army had consisted of forty-eight thousand (a point since ascertained), and that Joseph Buonaparte had been descried by one of Sir Arthur's staff.—The enemy sustained the loss of more than ten thousand men, with that of twenty pieces of brass cannon, and five standards.

We entered the field eighteen thousand three hundred strong; and our loss, as will appear by the following returns, fell very heavy, on the officers as well as privates.

	Killed	Wounded	Missing
General Staff	5	9	—
Lieut-Colonels	2	10	—
Majors	1	12	—
Captains	7	53	5
Lieutenants	15	71	3
Cornets and Ensigns	3	34	1
Adjutants	1	6	—
Serjeants	28	165	15
Drummers	4	16	9
Rank and File	735	3537	620
Total	801	3913	653

Recapitulation	
Killed	801
Wounded	3913
Missing	653
Grand Total	5367

The following is an abstract of the total loss of the respective regiments (including officers, non-commissioned officers and privates) in killed, wounded, and missing, in the battles of Talavera.

General Staff	14
3rd Dragoon Guards	3
4th Dragoons	12
14th Light Dragoons	16
16th *Ditto*	14
23rd *Ditto*	207
1st *Ditto* (German Legion)	42
Royal British Artillery	34
Royal German Artillery	34
Royal Engineers	2
Royal Staff Corps	2
1st Battalion Coldstream	297
1st Battalion 3rd Guards	322
3rd Foot	142
2nd Battalion 7th Foot	65
2nd *Ditto* 24th	355
1st *Ditto* 29th	180
2nd *Ditto* 31st	249
1st *Ditto* 40th	53
1st *Ditto* 45th	193
1st Battalion 48th	176
2nd *Ditto ditto*	71
2nd *Ditto* 53rd	39
5th *Ditto* 60th	77
1st *Ditto* 61st	272
2nd *Ditto* 68th	128
2nd *Ditto* 83rd	288
2nd *Ditto* 87th	253
1st *Ditto* 88th	140
1st *Ditto* 97th	52
1st *Ditto* Detachments	274

2nd *Ditto ditto*	21
1st Line Batt. German Legion	300
1st and 2nd Light Batt. *ditto*	79
2nd Line Batt. *ditto*	390
5th *Ditto ditto*	300
7th *Ditto ditto*	256
Total	5367

Before the morning of the 29th the enemy had effected their retreat beyond the Alberche; and our men were, during the day, busily employed in burying the dead, and conveying the wounded into the town. It is painful to record, that the streets still contained pitiable wretches, who had lain in torture during the night, mixed with the bodies of those who had expired. Some officers, on their return from exploring the field of battle, described the sight of dismembered limbs, embowelled and otherwise mangled bodies, as too horrible for contemplation; and even expressed their regret at having witnessed the scene.

30th.—Though the whole of the preceding day and night had been occupied in removing the wounded, several still remained amidst the slaughter: and their numbers were so considerable, in proportion to the surgeons, that many of those removed had not been dressed; and even several necessary amputations remained inevitably unperformed; whilst other sufferers were brought in throughout the day and night.

By the *31st* the French had retreated about two leagues; and our advanced posts were formed by General Craufurd's light brigade, and a troop of horse artillery, which had arrived from Lisbon on the 29th.

August 2.—This evening our army received orders to march at four o'clock the next morning; and on the 3rd fell back to Oropeza.

Confined to my bed since the 28th, I lost the pleasure of being with my regiment, and am precluded from giving a regular diary of its movements; it is, however, essential, briefly to state what became of the army. Sir Arthur, finding that Marshal Soult was in great force at Placentia, marched to Oropeza, with a view of attacking him; but finding that the Spanish army, which were left to cover our sick and wounded, had also retired on Oropeza, it was then found expedient to change the routes! and cross the Tagus at Puente del Arzobispo, and thus secure a retreat on Portugal.—Notwithstanding our videttes were, at one time, within a league of the enemy, he suffered them to pass unmolested; and our army effected a steady retreat; having previously sent on about two hundred cars, containing a part of the wounded, which were frequently stopped to throw off those who died on the road.

The army having reached its destination (in an exhausted state, from fatigue, and scarcity of provision), was stationed as follows:—Head-Quarters at Badajos;—General Sherbrooke's division from Lobau to Merida, with a German brigade of artillery at the former, and the troops of horse artillery, with some cavalry, at the latter place;—the light infantry brigade at Portalegre and Neisa; and some other brigades near Campo Mayor and Albuquerque;—four brigades of artillery encamped near Badajos; and the 40th Regiment in the town;—the light dragoons (nearly dismounted) at and near Villa Viçosa.—The sick were sent into hospital at Elvas; to which place the medical staff with the army, and those left at Lisbon, repaired.

3rd.—On the retreat of the army from Talavera I was left in bed, and remained uninformed of the circumstance till ten o'clock this day.—Soon after, a surgeon came, and consoled me by saying the French were not likely to return, and that our army had fallen back for the purpose of getting better supplies during their halt; but that, at all events, my attempting to move would be attended with the almost certainty of losing my life.—The surgeon had not left the room three hours, when my man ran in, to say the French were close to the town, and that everyone who was able to stir was making the best of his way to the rear. I had but a short time to take my choice of falling into the hands of the enemy a perfect cripple, or moving at the risk of dying on the road.

Preferring freedom to captivity, under any circumstances, I soon decided to attempt a retreat;—was then taken out of bed, and carried downstairs; and, with pillows fixed to the saddle, was just able to support myself on a horse,—my man leading him at a slow walk, under a broiling sun, towards Oropeza.—Before proceeding far in the town, I was informed that Calera was the point to which the sick were ordered: accordingly my march was directed for that place; whither there was little difficulty in finding my way, the road being soon crowded with wounded men. After having travelled a few miles, the pain occasioned by the motion of the horse was less acute; and by having recourse to a calabash of vinegar and water whenever I was likely to faint, I supported myself wonderfully well.—On reaching Calera, we found that Puente del Arzobispo was the place of destination for the sick; which occasioned my journey that night to be four leagues farther.

The other wounded men had got so far ahead, that I was several times near being lost on the heath, and with difficulty reached Arzobispo by eleven o'clock. The people were gone to bed, and only one light was to be seen. The *alcalde* (or constable) was soon found, who, after an apparent altercation with a woman, desired me to go into the cabin containing the light, and went away. On my approaching the door, the heroine flew at me like a tigress, with a patriot in her rear to support her. She positively refused admission, though she saw me in a fainting state, and knew my request was only for permission to lie on some straw in the passage.—During this squabble my head turned giddy, and had not my man supported me, I should have fallen off the horse. At this moment a dragoon came up, who, having his hands disengaged, soon put the patriot and his *señora* to flight, and helped me into the house. Here, laid on some straw by the side of a sick Spaniard, I remained the night. My other servants and horses were lost, and slept on the heath; but, by the greatest accident, found me out in the morning.

4th.—I was again put on horseback, at five o'clock a. m. On reaching the further end of the town, whence the sick were expected to proceed, they had not then received instructions, and were waiting the arrival of a field officer, who was deputed to take them in charge. I then entered another house, where, with some opposition, a mattress was got, on which I laid till a wounded officer came by, who was retreating with his family, and we proceeded together to Navallé Morelecho.

5th.—Continued our march to Lasteralia, where we rested, and had some tea.—On our way to this place the cart of my party broke down; and we were under the necessity of wait- ing till a car was pressed, and wild bullocks were driven from the mountains, to bring on the baggage.—All difficulties be- ing overcome, we proceeded. Faint with the heat of the day, I was obliged to be placed in a *calèche*; and the road being one of the roughest that ever wheels travelled, I was in torture the whole way. The hip bone, which a rifle-ball had gone through and shattered, and the muscles of my back, where it was then lodged, were bumped with the greatest violence against the hard sides of the carriage; and my riding on horseback again that day was totally out of the question, as the pain suffered already had made me so weak I could not have supported myself.—At last, we reached a village, the name of which (I believe) is Moyathis. Here we passed the night.

6th.—The carriage-road extending no farther than this place, my friends were obliged to return all the way back to Arzobispo; and were almost in the face of the French *videttes*, who very soon after drove the Spaniards from that place. I determined on continuing through the mountains, and travelling (so long as life permitted me) on a small mule. My object was to make for Truxillo: as, if the army were suffered to retire unmolested; or, on the other hand, held the enemy in check; the odds were, that, by a forced march, I could reach the point before them: and if compelled to a precipitate retreat, I must at all events be made prisoner.—I then started, taking my chance whether Truxillo would be found occupied by French or British troops.

This day (being joined by a wounded officer of infantry) we

began to encounter the passes of the Guadeloupe Mountains. Here we went sometimes over solid rocks, where our mules were every moment stumbling; and at others over the roughest stones, interspersed with deep holes: then down descents of heights, where the animals could scarcely keep on their legs: and occasionally travelling the sides of precipices, by the mere pass of a goat-track:—a pleasant situation for a man with an empty stomach and broken bones!!!—We had a guide, or never should have been able to make out the passes; and the whole country being uninhabited[15], we could have found no one to direct us.— After a broiling and exhausting march, we late at night reached Allia; where we had to wait a long time before there could be got a billet.

7th.—Continued our march to Logrosan; and on the 8th to Solita. Here they would neither give nor sell us anything, till we made them understand that I was a brigadier of cavalry, and that my troops were coming in the next day; who, if our requisitions were refused, I would order to take the *alcalde* prisoner, and send him to England.—On this we had brought us the produce of the village, with a thousand apologies, and benefited by a great deal oppressed civility.

9th.—Arrived at Truxillo, where we were cheered by the sight of English soldiers, and found ourselves two leagues in rear of the British army.

This town brings you again into the road from Madrid to Lisbon. It is a large place, torn to pieces by the French: has some good houses; and is famous for having given birth to Pizarro.

During our pass through this desert country, we were literally starving, and had the utmost difficulty in procuring bread, even at an imposing price: as to wine or spirits, they were not to be heard of; and there was scarcely a bit of meat to be bought. Our horses and mules, which were chiefly fed with stale chaff, were nearly famished, as well as ourselves. For my own part, I believe

---

15. A region destitute of every living creature, except a number of Spanish cavalry by whom we were nearly rode over.

my life was owing to the goats: their owners, the patriots, refusing to sell me a little milk, I contrived to get this nourishment by stealth; making the guide fill my bottle every day, when we came to a herd of these animals.—To complete this wretched retreat, we were everywhere annoyed with fleas, bugs, and body lice,

10th.—Proceeded on my journey, passing through Santa Cruz; and, after a hard and hot day's march, arrived at Meajados; where, what with fasting and fatigue, I was ready to drop from the mule. We found the people in this place (if possible) more uncivil than at others[16]: my servants were an hour before they could get a billet; during which time I was laid on the pavement, where the patriots refused me even a pillow, and with the greatest reluctance brought out a little water. A mob had soon assembled round me, poking in their stinking heads as if a basket of cheap fish were selling in the street.—At last I got into the house of one of the *Junta*, who fully answered my expectations!

11th.—At seven in the evening, having hired mules to carry my men, two of whom had been forced to walk the whole journey with their feet quite raw, I continued my march; and by three in the morning reached Santo Padro; where I saw a light at a post-house, begged admission, and was laid on a mattress for an hour,—Having then sufficiently recruited myself, I started for Merida, and arrived at seven o'clock; making my march exactly twelve hours.

On entering this place, the traveller is presented with fine ruins of an aqueduct; near which there is, still passable, a Roman bridge.—Merida contains an ancient temple, formerly dedicated to Mars, but since devoted to Christian worship; also a subter-

---

16. A brother officer, who was dangerously ill of a fever brought on by travelling with a severe wound, was here laid on the floor of a room, while his servant went for medical assistance. The man, having no safer place to deposit his mister's baggage, laid it somewhere near him: the patriots, taking advantage of the man's absence and, the officer's situation, carried a great part of it off; robbing him, not only of his helmet and appointments (the very articles used in defence of their country), but of several things which, from being a cripple, he more particularly required.—The same officer met with similar treatment at other places.

raneous tunnel, leading from the river.

I was here billeted in the house of a *Donna*, who told us she was the wife of a brigadier. Being in much want of sleep. I was immediately put to bed; but had scarcely got warm, when myriads of—I knew not what—were crawling over me. By making a great effort, I raised myself sufficiently to throw off the bedclothes, and found them to be bugs. Being unable to help myself, I began bawling, and at last was heard; taken out of bed; and stuck up in an armchair, till another *casâ* was provided.

13th.—We rested here during this day; but not wishing to pass another night in the place, I purposed starting in the cool of the evening. Finding myself very weak, from excessive fatigue and having my rest interrupted, I attempted to hire a car, but without success. My landlady, who showed a great deal of pretended civility, and affected to pity me extremely, assured me there was no sort of conveyance to be had, and expressed her regret at having nothing of that kind to offer. Shortly after, a large car, with two fine mules, came to the door, and was unloaded of sacks.

In the meantime my fellow-traveller hobbled off to the *alcalde*; got a warrant to press the same; and we detained it in our possession. This machine proved to be the property of the old woman, who became so enraged, that her palaver burst into the furies of a vixen.—We then procured asses for our men, and at eleven at night got our convoy under way: at one, in the afternoon of the 14th, we arrived at Badajos. Having got into a billet I sent for the car-driver, to remunerate him for his trouble, and pay for his expenses back to Merida; but he had saved me this cost, by decamping with his car and mules the moment my men had left him—I suppose, through fear of his getting pressed into Portugal.

My situation prevented me from seeing anything of Badajos, or indeed of other places, further than what was presented to my view while I passed by. This city I observed to be eminently situated, and on the south of the Guadiana: it is strongly fortified, and the frontier town next Portugal; to reach which you pass the

Guadiana by a fine Roman bridge considerably more than one-third of a mile in length.

15th.—Hired a *calèche*, and went to Elvas[17].—On our entering Portugal from Spain, the sudden transition from haughtiness to civility is scarcely to be credited. On being interrogated by the guard, which is usual in a frontier town, I remained in the street, while my servant went to General Leita, the Commandant and Governor, to inform him who I was, and explain my situation. He immediately sent down his brigade-major, with directions to assist me, and to show me every kind of attention.—I was conducted to a princely billet, in the house of a *Donnana Fortunata*; where I received great kindness, and had every luxury brought to my bedside, with the attendance of two servants.

The general did me the honour to send his nephew, with his compliments, offering anything I might want: and on hearing I had expressed a wish to hire a conveyance for the next day, he insisted on my taking his carriage, and using it as far as I thought proper;—a liberality of conduct perfectly according with General Leita's well-known character.

On the morning of the 16th, the carriage and four, with three servants, drove up to the gate, while we were partaking of an excellent breakfast, which had been prepared for us before daylight.— About half past five we started; and while passing out of the garrison the respect paid us was very entertaining. By natives hat in hand, and guards turning out, we received every mark of honour that could be shown a Prince.

We soon reached Estramos, where we were received by a Portuguese orderly, whom the general had sent on to provide a billet.

17th.—Being greatly recruited by our comparatively easy mode of travelling the preceding day, we took leave of our fine

---

17. This city, with its grand aqueduct and cistern, fortifications, convents, academy, churches, &c. I regret having been unable to survey; and have here again to apologize for the deficiency of my narrative; for I am particularly, unwilling to supply the defect of my own observation by reference to travels or history of the country.

equipage, and proceeded to Arrayolos.

18th.—Passed Monté Mornovo, and reached Vendas Nova: where, at first, we could get no cover for ourselves or horses—the *juis de foro* (or constable) being at Lisbon, and the natives refusing to admit us without an order. We soon settled this point, by selecting the best *casâ* we could find, and forcing a billet. The house we were in was contiguous to a long range of buildings which formed an ancient royal residence. This, we were told, the Prince Regent occasionally used as a hunting seat.

19th.—Went through Peagones and Rilvas, and arrived at Aldea Galega; where we most heartily rejoiced, having accomplished the last stage of our truly miserable and tormenting journey.

20th.—We embarked in a large boat, which, in an hour and a half, sailed across the Tagus, and brought us to the quay at Lisbon.—The man we had sent forward to provide for us, having been so long on short allowance, that, according to the old excuse, half a pint got in his head, was neither to be seen nor heard of.

After lying for three hours in the boat, and being surveyed by a staring multitude (like a fresh-caught sturgeon by the Cockneys, on the banks of the Thames), I gave up entering a billet for that day, and was taken to Owen's hotel.

Our happy transmigration, which we performed in eighteen days, amounted to eighty-eight leagues,.—Their leagues are rated at about four and one-fifth English miles, though many of them far exceed that distance.

The number of leagues between each place are as follow:—

Spain.	
From Talavera de la Reyna to:	Leagues.
Puente del Arzobispo	7
Navallé Morelecho	2
Moyathis	4
Allia	5
Logrosan	5

Solita	4
Truxillo - On the great road from Madrid to Lisbon	5
Meajados - *ditto*	6
Merida - *ditto*	8
Badajos - *ditto*	9
Portugal.	
Elvas - On the great road from Madrid to Lisbon	3
Estramos - *ditto*	6
Arrayolos - *ditto*	6
Vendas Novas - *ditto*	7
Aldea Galega - *ditto*	8
Passage to Lisbon	3
Total	88

Probably I should never have surmounted this journey, had it not been for repeated fomentations of hot water on my first arrival at each place; which, by counteracting any additional inflammation that might have been brought on from exertion, enabled me to proceed. The pain, nevertheless, was incessant; and, from being teased with flies by day and vermin by night, I could not get the necessary rest even for a person in health. This, added to the scarcity of almost everything I could eat, had reduced me to a perfect skeleton.

22nd.—I was removed to an excellent billet.

In a few days after, all these exertions began to operate on my health; and the heat of the season greatly tended to increase the illness. The weather, which had for some time been intensely hot, then became intolerable; and the evenings so close as to be quite oppressive. We were obliged to remain almost suffocated, from having the windows shut, to avoid letting in myriads of gnats and other insects, that would have tormented us during the night. My sickness soon increased to that degree as to prevent my taking any nourishment; and my wound became so incessantly painful as, in spite of opiates, to deprive me of sleep almost every night

I lodged in the house of a lady of distinction, to whom I consider myself much indebted for her most polite attention. It was the study of this lady to make me as comfortable as my infirmity

74

would admit of, and procure for me everything I could wish: in both, she amply succeeded, having an establishment where nothing could be wanting.

September 14.—Continued very ill. After losing a fortnight of my leave, waiting for a conveyance to England, I learnt that a fleet of empty transports were ordered to sail for Portsmouth, under convoy of the *Emerald* frigate. I had the good fortune to get a passage; for procuring which I am under many obligations to my hostess, and also for the kindest exertion on the part of the British Minister. Having my choice of the fleet, I fixed on a ship which had good accommodation for myself and horses, and what is not readily to be met with, a very pleasant and obliging man for a captain,

15th.—Being informed that the convoy were likely to sail early the next morning, at two this afternoon I dispatched a soldier with baggage, in a Portuguese boat.—This man was directed to bring back with him, immediately, the ship's longboat, so as to embark my horses before sunset; but he never returned; and I, expecting him every moment, delayed sending after him till it was too late to get a boat. The night was thus passed in suspense.

16th.—Early this morning I was roused out of bed, by being told that the fleet were on the point of sailing, and the ship's boat was waiting for me. I was carried out, half undressed, and, when in the act of getting into the boat, with my mind made up to the loss of all my baggage, the dragoon who had taken it made, his appearance, informing me it was safely deposited on board.—It seemed this man had had a narrow escape.

On his returning the preceding evenings there came on so hard a gale that the boat and crew were nearly swamped, and had been drifted to the opposite side of the Tagus, where they lay out all night. I then had my horses galloped to Lisbon, directing the men, who went with them, to offer any price for a boat and attempt (what I despaired of) getting them on board.

This was so well managed, that they arrived almost immediately after me, and were embarked when we were in the very act of getting under weigh. I then, notwithstanding this hurry, brought off everything, but my stock of live poultry, which was left behind through the stupidity—or, perhaps, kept behind, through the cunning—of a blundering Irish dragoon.

About eleven o'clock we sailed out of the Tagus with a northerly breeze, working to westward for a good offing and the chance of another wind.

17th and *18th*.—The wind continued unfavourable.

19th.—This day, when finding myself almost at the point of death for want of surgical assistance, there occurred for me a most providential circumstance:—It suddenly came on so calm, that boats could pass from ship to ship, and. the commodore very kindly came alongside, to offer anything he had that I might want I requested the attendance of his surgeon, who was immediately put on board.

After examining, my wound, he sent the boat back for his assistant and instruments, and opened the muscles of my back, where it, was probable a mortification would speedily have taken place; and had not this operation been performed, I should have died on the voyage.—I became so faint that they were obliged to postpone doing anything farther that day: from what was effected, I found almost immediate relief.

In the evening there came on a light breeze, fair for England.

20th.—The surgeons came on board again, and with some difficulty extracted the ball, which had been considerably flattened by passing through the muscles and bone.

The kindness of our commodore cannot pass unobserved, and will by me be ever remembered with gratitude. In addition to every possible attention paid me during the voyage, he sent over sea-stock enough for half the ship's company, begging me to ask for anything I might happen to fancy.

21st—The wind increased, and blew directly fair for England.—

We this day entered the Bay of Biscay, where we ran nine knots an hour, during the night, under very little sail.

22nd, 23rd, and *24th.*—The wind continued very fair.—In order to keep well clear of Ushant, we steered a westerly course, sailing some distance in the Atlantic.

25th.—Opened the Channel; and at nine o'clock a. m. the ship's carpenter got his glass of grog, for first discovering the Lizard Point—We soon passed Falmouth, briskly scudding up Channel.

26th.—We had very little wind till the afternoon, when a fine breeze sprung up, and soon brought us in sight of the Isle of Wight; and about eight that evening we dropped anchor at Spithead.

It blew a hurricane all night, and we were at one time in great danger. A large ship, having broke her cable, came down with wind and tide, and got foul of us about midnight.

Diary of our Passage from Lisbon to Spithead.	
From midday on Saturday to	Miles in 24 hours,
Midday on Sunday 17th	81
.... 18th	83
.... 19th	61
.... 20th	93
.... 21st	51
.... 22nd	138
.... 23rd	168
.... 24th	151
.... 25th	162
.... 26th	140
Total made good	1128

N. B. Taking the chart in a direct line crossing Cape Finisterre, we made the distance 704 miles.

27th.—It blew so hard all the morning, that even the sailors would not venture in a boat. I remained imprisoned in the cabin, with stale provision, tantalised by viewing the Land of Luxury from the window; and with so little hope of getting on shore, that my mind was reconciled to lying with my sore sides another night on hard boards. In the evening, however, though still very rough, the wind rather abated, and I was determined to complete my emancipation. The ship continued rolling to that degree it was impossible to let me down alongside; but I was lowered aft, in the stern-boat, which I expected every moment would turn upside down, and empty out me and my personal property, like the contents of a Lisbon *garret-pail*. However, as in other narrow escapes, I came off well; and, having surmounted every danger and difficulty with the most providential success, landed safe in the most enviable island under Heaven!

Alter feasting on an English dinner at Portsmouth, I set off in a chaise, which literally appeared to fly after the crawling conveyances of Spain and Portugal.

On the 28th (the very day two months from the battle of Talavera) I happily reached my final destination. Such has been my situation, that it has necessarily occasioned me, in the foregoing pages, to appear more of the egotist than might be wished; but, for the narrative to be at all connected, it was scarcely to be avoided, and was perhaps the least evil that could be adopted.

By having recounted a few well-testified anecdotes of the Spaniards, I do not mean to assert that there are none of their nation who look upon a British soldier with esteem; but the fact intended to be here established is—that it was not my good fortune to behold any trace of kindness towards us: on the contrary, in all places, apathy; in some, a seemingly confirmed disgust.

Campaigns in
Portugal and Spain

William Graham

Contents

Advertisement

After a slumber of ages, and an abject submission to a yoke of priest-craft which degraded the Spanish name below the standard of the human character, Spain has assumed an imposing attitude, which renders every fact connected with that country deeply interesting to the whole civilized world.

The Editor of this Journal has therefore great satisfaction in submitting to his readers two original works on Spain—one performed by a gentleman connected with the Commissariat attached to the British army in the late war, and the other a Sketch of the state of Spain on certain interesting points, but valuable as the result of recent observation.

Neither of them were written for the public eye, but on that account they will be deemed more valuable; because it too often happens that Travels written for publication, are accommodated to public prejudices, and assume a formality of style and manner incompatible with the pleasure afforded by this species of composition, when it results from the unsophisticated feelings of the writer, derived from local circumstances.

These works being preferred on account of their temporary interest, Pertusier's Travels round Constantinople, and some other important works in preparation, are deferred for another month.

Arrangements are making to introduce some of the late Travels in Egypt, which have led to so many' very interesting discoveries in the antiquities of that country; and the Editor hopes to be able, within three or four months, to lay before his readers (he result of the pending Voyage in the region of Baffin's Bay.

London, June 10, 1820.

Campaigns in Portugal and Spain

In the month of October, 1812, I bid *adieu* to my father and old friends, and stepped into the mail coach, in College Green, Dublin, for Cork. Here I fell asleep with regretful ruminations, it being the first time in my life that I had ever travelled.

I was supported in the trial of this separation, by the prospect of gratifying my curiosity in seeing foreign countries, and acting my part under Lord Wellington. I considered myself as now beginning the world on my own account, and I indulged in the hopes of becoming a more useful member of society, and eventually of relating my adventures, on my return home, to all my friends, around the Vicar of Wakefield's fire-side.

We arrived in the morning, about eight o'clock, at Kilkenny, where we were much enlivened by a good cheerful fire and breakfast. I travelled inside, yet found it very cold, and one of the outside passengers was nearly frozen to death during the night. Kilkenny coal emits no smoke, and, when lighted, which takes more trouble than the common coal, it produces a very strong heat, and leaves no ashes. After breakfast, we again went into the coach, and I was not a little amused at observing the delightful country we passed through. There were many passengers who came and went during the day, but they were all silent, except one man, who talked like a parrot, for his tongue never ceased from the time he came into the coach until he left it. He dwelt much on the mail being robbed, and assured us it was likely to be our case. This he seemed to enjoy, so that one would have thought he wished it. "As soon as night fell, perhaps some troop of *banditti* would start out from the road side and attack us." In consequence, I kept a good look out for every clump of trees that grew near the road side (as Ireland had been much disturbed of late) and my fancy would sometimes picture their hats moving among the trees.

A story which he told us seemed to alarm the other passengers, particularly as we were hastening to the very place where the robbery happened. The coach carrying the mail, about two years ago, accompanied by twenty dragoons, had gone on very well, until the dragoons, who were first, were suddenly dismounted, by the horses tumbling over a rope tied across the road. The dragoons, little accustomed to be unhorsed in this secret way, were alarmed, and a shot being fired in amongst them, they took to their heels, leaving their horses behind, together with their commanding officer, who fainted away with fright. The guard being next shot at, was wounded, and contrived to limp away with the coachman, who, in his account of the enemy, magnified them to four hundred men, completely equipped, with hats towering like a church steeple. Now our informer, to prove the genius of his countrymen, reported that it had all been contrived by a single man, with fifteen or twenty hats placed on a wall; he had three or four pistols, which he fired alternately from behind the hats, as if a body of men were really firing.

The coachman seeing this, concluded that a party of the rebels were there concealed, and reported accordingly. The robber, of course, had sufficient time to plunder everything; but what became of the passengers we were not told. We kept a good lookout for the wall, which we safely passed, and I thought it might have been a well-chosen place to make such an attempt, as the wall was twelve or thirteen feet above the road, and the ground inside not more than four or five feet from the top of the wall: however, we arrived, at seven o'clock, safe at Clonmell.

At the second stage from Clonmell, we came to Fermoy, one of the handsomest towns, perhaps, in Europe. It was principally laid out and built by a Mr. Anderson, Banker and Architect, and who, I am since informed, has much improved it. About ten o'clock at night, we arrived at Cork, winding delightfully along the river Lee for some miles. Cork is 120 frisk miles from Dublin, and we were twenty-six hours on the road; the roads were very good the whole distance, but the times for breakfast and dinner were badly regulated; for, though we breakfasted at eight in the morning, we did not dine, or halt anywhere to refresh, until seven in the evening.

At Fermoy I had met my friend, Mr. David Gordon, one of the assistant surgeons of the regiment I was going to join. We afterwards kept company all the way, until our arrival on board the *Alfred*. Next morning, I went out to see the captain, and find out an old friend, Mr. T., with whom I went to change my money for Spanish dollars. This I did at 6s. 3d. each, by which I lost 1s. 9d in every dollar. Here I must observe, to the disgrace of our moralization, that those are most imposed who have the least protection. It is a blemish in the character of Cork and other sea-port towns, that we must submit to the money-changers, who will give for dollars five shillings apiece, and sell them again at a most enormous profit. This is a particular hardship on the soldier, who must take money with him wherever he is going, where another person can take goods. To a mercantile man it will often be a gain, instead of a loss. In fact, where men have been fighting hard, or in danger of their lives at every step, their comforts should be made more on an equality with the rest of the community; but the very reverse is the case.

In the afternoon, Gordon and I went down to Cove, eight or nine miles from Cork; it is situated on an island, and is the general rendezvous for ships of war. We arrived at seven o'clock in the evening, having walked through a country, the scenery of which is beautiful. Here we found at an hotel several officers of the 20th. Colonel Ross was to command the land forces, which were composed of the Sixth and Twentieth regiments. Having arrived on board the *Alfred*, a seventy-four gun ship, armed *en flute*, we sent word to Colonel Ross, then at supper. He appointed us to the *Dover*, of twenty-four guns. Here, for want of room, I was obliged to have my bed in Captain Russell's cabin: he was very friendly to me, as were all the other officers. I slept but little, not being accustomed to the rolling of a ship, and my thoughts occupied with the immense size of the *Alfred* and the *Regulus*, a sixty-four, with their large guns run out at the port-holes.

Next morning early I mounted up to the quarter-deck to look round me, and seeing a gentleman in a blue coat, I took him for a midshipman, and entered freely into conversation with him, and he with me. I asked him several questions relative to the navy, all of which he answered with great good humour. After breakfast, I again went on deck, when I saw this supposed midshipman come out of his cabin in full navy uniform, two epaulettes, and a cross on his breast. I was, of course, surprised to find him the captain of our vessel. He then gave his orders to clear the pennants, which was done in a moment, like clockwork. This was for making signals. Then be ordered two sailors before, for having struck each other. This was preparatory to some hard duty. He also gave notice, before all the crew, that if men fell out amongst each other, or had any cause of complaint, they should report it, and not revenge their own wrongs, so as to be both judges and executioners. In short, if he ever again found any man to strike another, he would order him to be soundly flogged; but in this instance be was lenient, from its being the first offence. The captain, concluded by adding, that any complaint should be properly investigated, and the injured party indemnified as far as possible. The whole crew seemed perfectly contented at the justness of this proceeding.

It was evident that his men were fond of him: one of the sailors told me afterwards that he had sailed nineteen years under him, and never knew him to punish a man without the crew being convinced of the justice of it, nor did he ever punish cruelly. He was, however, when necessity compelled, very strict, and then he punished with severity. This kind of management made him respected and beloved, both by those who were under his command, and those who were merely lookers on. His orders' were obeyed with alacrity, more from esteem for his character than from fear. Many of our navy officers, I am sorry to say, tyrannize over their men, so that they tremble at an order, and fear actually prevents, in some degree, the punctual execution of it; whereas, on board this ship, every command was obeyed with ease, and the duty of the ship moved forward without noise or confusion, just as if no order had been given:

My baggage not having arrived, I was obliged to go on shore, and during my absence the fleet sailed, which put me to a serious inconvenience. I was in a lonely situation, without one single individual that I knew, and having changed my dollars at Cork for 6s 3d apiece, I was obliged to pay them away here at 5s each. I met here, however, a friendly man, formerly a chief magistrate in Jamaica: he had been a planter, and, although nearly sixty years of age, he had come to Ireland, to marry a sister of Lord N. He was now on his return to Jamaica, to dispose of his property, meaning to live in Ireland with his young wife. He was very rich, and paid eighty guineas for his passage. I often dined on board his ship, with the captain, who invited me. Here I also met with an officer named Wrixon, and his family, who was going to Quebec to join his regiment, the 98th Foot. Lieutenant W. went every day to Cork, and I was frequently invited to dinner with him. They were, indeed, a happy and virtuous family.

Cove is pleasantly situated on an island, facing the entrance of the harbour, which is defended by Camden and Carlisle forts, one on each side. Spike Island, almost in the mouth of the entrance, would blow any enemy's ship out of the water, as it is well defended with four hundred great guns, and others were adding to it when I left it. This harbour, which is the general rendezvous for all ships and fleets bound westward, is sufficient to contain more than a thousand sail, with depth of water for any size. I met here an old school-fellow, going out as a volunteer after the 6th Foot. His name was M. His brother Ralph was then a lieutenant in it.

Having been delayed near a fortnight. Cox and I were ordered on board a transport bound for Lisbon. She was a large ship of four hundred tons, and commanded by a tyrant of a captain, who ever flogged his men unmercifully, but particularly his cabin boy. Here we laid in a stock for ourselves, of biscuit, coffee, sugar, butter, &c. but took no meat, as our rations were thought sufficient, all of us liking salt meat, and expecting to make the run to Lisbon in seven days.

Being now on board a large and roomy ship, I proceeded to take a view of my companions. There was Lieutenant Cox, of the Rifle Corps, returning to join his regiment in Spain, having just recovered from a severe wound in his arm; R. a volunteer for any regiment that would take him: he was a rough Irish lad, of good family, with some money, and a letter of recommendation from the Marquis of Waterford to Marshal Beresford. Also Mrs. H., Miss H., and two children. Mrs. H. was the wife of a quarter-master in the fusiliers, but though he did not wish her to run the dangerous chances of war, natural affection led her to make this voyage to join him.

1812. *Nov. 5.*—We sailed out of Cove Harbour at one o'clock, under a grand salute of twenty-one guns from every fort and ship of war in the harbour. The compliment was not in honour of us, but from its being the anniversary of the gunpowder plot. Towards night we lost sight of land, and I was highly amused at surveying the rocky coast of Ireland. It seemed curious to me, that shipping could find out the entrance of Cove Harbour. I could see no mark to steer by, the mouth or entrance being only a mile wide. As night advanced, I viewed the receding shore with a degree of regret no pen can describe. A melancholy gloom had likewise spread over all the soldiers, except those who had been abroad before. The inhabitants of Spitzbergen prefer their horrid country and half-starved condition, to any other in the world. Custom, however, wears away the regret of leaving it, and life is supported by a power, Hope, without which, man would sink, as it were, to a nonentity.

As the night fell, our spirits gradually lowered, and all was silence, except the whistling of the wind in the shrouds, and the cursing of the Captain. Such delights altogether prevented us from sleeping this night.

Nov. 6.—This morning the weather was fair, and I had leisure to count the number of ships in the fleet. These, amounting to thirty sail, were under the convoy of a frigate of forty-four guns. Mrs. H. went to bed, when she got on board, very ill, and never recovered till we came within view of Belem Castle, near Lisbon. Our principal amusement on board was playing draughts, and everyone being sick, except Cox and I, we used to sit at this game for hours together. I was frequently amused at seeing the porpoises tumbling and rolling about; but could never penetrate one of them with a musket ball, though I hit several.

We now lived principally on biscuits buttered, and coffee; but the greatest relish was a dish of potatoes; these we purchased from the carpenter daily, who had laid in an ample provision. Poor R. was taken very ill, and we had but little mirth or wit, as all were sick about us. On the seventh of November, the wind changed directly in our teeth, and now our real troubles were to begin.

On the night of the seventh of November, the wind rose to a perfect hurricane, so as effectually to drown the noise of our cursing captain, who, however, gave the men two or three drams a piece. From this time, sleep and I parted, till our arrival on shore. The dismal noise in the rigging reverberated as if against a forest, in one continued roar. The waves came rolling towards us, in mountains piled on each other; the sea appeared white as snow, and we could hardly see the illumination of the ship cutting the water, unless by the brightness from the white foam, which gave a partial lustre to the scene. When the lightning ceased, the tremendous thunder which accompanied it, stunned our ears, till the sounds seemed to roll, at last, to some other world. One of the flashes struck the water, close by us, and disappeared, leaving, in appearance. a thick vapour after it. We could do nothing but look on, and hold firm to the ship's sides; this was preferable to lying in bed, where one could have no comfort. The straining of the ship's timbers, continually creaking, as she rolled from side to side, we all preferred the deck to the cabin. The rain came down in torrents, and the lightning, when taking leave of us, seemed to set the whole atmosphere in a blaze, so that we could distinctly see as in the daytime.

I now found what an excellent seaman our captain was; he certainly kept the ship steady, when he directed the helm, and he, with the mate, who, by the bye, would joke with him now and then on his temper, kept watch about. In such a time, the wrong direction of the helm would have sunk the vessel, and now it required quick work to alter the windlass, on such a dark and tempestuous night, where hardly the oldest sailor could keep his feet.

On the morning of the eighth, the captain told as we were in the Atlantic, approaching the Bay of Biscay. While he was speaking, the ship made a heel, and going almost on her side, I lost my hold, and was driven with amazing force against the capstern, and from thence to the other side of the ship against one of the main beams. It proved my protection from the sea, for had I been driven against the beading only, it must have given way, and I should have been plunged into the abyss, without the most distant probability of succour. The captain was quite surprised when he found I was not dead; my head and shoulder were severely cut, and bled preciously; but they did not occasion any pain, after being dressed, and I was well in a few days.

Next day, the weather cleared a little, but our captain was nearly put beside himself, when he saw Cox and I bit down to draughts. He insisted we should throw them overboard; we demurred; he begged, entreated, and would have used violence, if he durst; but, seeing his agitation, we complied, highly amused to think, that the greatest brutes and tyrants are often the most pusillanimous. We continued our course, as well as constantly tacking could do it, until the tenth, when we were able to take an observation, the sun appearing at intervals.

We determined to make much of this day, having been nearly starved for want of our dinners, every day, which, however, it was impossible for anyone to get ready. So to work we fell, to assist the cook; but, when dinner was brought in, we found ourselves unable to keep the things on the table, and, at one swing of the vessel, our soup, that had cost us so much pains, was thrown off the table. We contrived to save the meat, and sat on the chairs which were lashed to the cabin floor: we held by them for fear of being upset, but R.'s chair suddenly giving way, hit the table so hard, that it knocked all the things off, so that plates, glasses, and tureens, all went smash in one universal wreck. The captain cursed us for our awkwardness, but, having his own plate between his knees, while endeavouring to save a decanter of brandy, he suddenly lost his hold, and all his service went in the same way. We had now fairly the laugh at him;—however, to make up matters, he treated us with a bottle of excellent Malaga wine, and so we parted for that time.

On the morning of the twelfth, we observed the frigate of which we were in charge, crowding all sail. We concluded she was going to leave us, but our captain cleared up this point, She had made signals to keep close together, which imported that an enemy was in view. In about an hour she was out of sight; though not half the sails were set that any of our fleet had, at twelve o'clock we came up with her and another ship; they were lying to; the stranger proved to be a friend. I was not a little astonished at the distance sailors can see at sea, for they bad made the discovery a full hour before we could espy them, even with glasses. When we joined them, the stranger went his own course, and we continued ours,

On the morning of the fifteenth, we had a glimpse of the coast of Spain, and, in the afternoon, could see the entrance to Corunna. At first, the coast appeared as a mist on the edge of the horizon; afterwards, it assumed a blueish hue, and seemed to be rising, as we approached nearer. We could distinguish the broken mountains, and at last the trees, houses, &c. And now the wind having, to our great joy, shifted to the north-east, we ran before it, till the morning of the 17th, when we came within view of the Rock of Lisbon, which at first seemed to be only a blue speck. We had lost sight of the fleet, some days before, but now fell in with numbers of shipping crowding in and out of the Tagus. As we approached the shore, we found it adorned with villages that looked delightful; the convents appeared beautiful beyond anything I could have imagined, and we might indistinctly mark the oranges on the trees. To add to all this, the day was fine and the weather inviting. We had asked the captain, on coming in view of the rock, whether we should be able to breakfast on shore; he thought we might; we were, however, so long in turning round the rock, that we gave up the idea, but determined to dine on shore, if possible.

And now I was completely gratified with everything I beheld; we took up a pilot, as usual, and the boat that he came in was the first thing that riveted our observation. It was very large and shaped like a canoe, sharp at both ends; it rose eight or ten feet out of the water, being turned in like the head of a fiddle, and the cut-water dotted with large inch-headed nails which stuck out above an inch and a half. This cut-water went up to the top of both fiddle-heads. The boat might contain about thirty men; it was painted with many gay colours, and sailed with a rapidity I had not witnessed before. One of these pilot-boats was in danger of being lost, very near us, among the breakers, but they hauled down their sail just in time, when not more than five or six yards from them. When they saw themselves running among the breakers, the boatmen set up the most frightful cries.

This sand-bank lies opposite to the mouth of the river, and is, probably, formed by the mud which is brought down, as is usual, coming in contact with the ocean. When we passed it, we came round by Fort St. Julian and Bougie; the last situated on a sand-bank in the river. It is shaped much like one of our Martello towers. Fort St. Julian can boast of a very strong battery, but it appears to be the only defence of the harbour. The city of Lisbon was about eight miles up the river, with Belem Castle projecting into the river. Buenos Ayres, the highest part of Lisbon, now appeared a sort of magnificent crest, and the landscape from this place was enchanting. Lisbon rose like an amphitheatre, from the side of the river.

Here and there, the eye would single out their convents, particularly one or two on the banks of the river.

At length, having turned to go up the river, we lost the advantage of the wind, which now blew directly in our teeth, and we were obliged to tack all the way, till we dropped anchor about three in the afternoon, before Belem Castle. In our tacking, we had the misfortune to be run foul of by another ship, which, indeed, had nearly sunk us; but we were not unrevenged, for the other ship's bowsprit was broken in the slings, and all her guns at that side that hit us were broken, from their lashings. We could see them rolling about, to the no small vexation and danger of the crew.

Having now ordered a boat alongside, we went into her, with our baggage, and rowed down to Lisbon, a distance of about two miles. I was surprised at seeing such a number of windmills on the right bank; I think I might say, without exaggeration, there were three hundred. It was a truly pleasant evening, the sun shining, and the temperature as warm as it is in England, in August. The wind had ceased, and the sunbeams reflected on the small waves, quivered in consonance with their undulations. It proved to be Sunday, and all the Portuguese were apparelled in their best costume. Our boat rode close along shore; every fresh object was amusing; but among all the people, we could see no one waiting to receive us, as we were strangers, and we were obliged to shift for ourselves as well as we could.

We arrived at last in Lisbon, and comfortable it was to get from the ship on dry land again. When we came to take our luggage out of the boat, not fewer than one hundred hungry Portuguese came and actually tore it out of our hands to carry it. We were obliged to put up with this rough demeanour: those wretches put me in mind of the *Lazzaroni* of Naples; their cut-throat looks were sure to make us civil. When they had deposited everything in a safe place, we gladly paid them a *Crusado Novo,* (two shillings and sixpence,) to get rid of them. We next repaired to a hotel kept by one Joze, in Rua das Flores, No. 83, where Cox had been before. The ladies could not be admitted, and were accommodated in another hotel, which we were glad of, and took our leave accordingly, as they had been but indifferent company, and shewed few tokens of polite conversation or education. Miss K— was the best behaved. Mrs. K. had only got out of bed this day, having never quitted her berth, (a small closet out of the main cabin) since we left Ireland. Miss K. often joined our coffee parties on deck, when the weather was agreeable. She was a little lump of fat, and would have liked Cox, but he did not seem to relish her endearments, so that we parted without reluctance, and we neither saw nor heard of them after.

On my arrival in the streets of the capital, I found myself much disappointed: nothing to be seen but narrow, dirty, crooked; streets, with no sideways for foot passengers. As the city is built on a hill, many of the streets are steep, and some have steps up them. The houses are seven or eight stories high, and the finest apartments are generally at the top; the ground floors in most of the houses being stables or shops, &c. In the streets, the sensations are perfectly disgusted, on account of the dirt, and filth being emptied out of the windows at night. I have frequently run the risk of some disagreeable reencounters, only escaping by exertion and forecast, as my billet lay two miles from our mess, in Largo das des Olarias. On my returning at night, I used frequently to hear the windows opened, and the cries "*Agoa Via*," a signal to those below to take care of their heads from the rain, &c. above. This filthy custom is kept up, I am told, in Edinburgh; but it makes the streets intolerably offensive, and most especially in a warm climate. There are few, if any, employed to remove this filth; the heavy rains, which are frequent here, as in all warm climates, being looked for to do the duty.

The water is carried about on men's heads, and sold, a quarter cask, or nine gallons, for a *vintin*, or 1½d. The Portuguese are remarkably dirty; few of the rooms have any fire place, the climate being hot enough without them. Charcoal is in general use for cooking, and this gives the air a peculiar and sulphurous smell. In their eating-houses, for the lower classes, their fish are fried on a moveable fire-place outside the door: their fish are *sardinias,* not half as big as our herrings; and, with some wine and *Agoa dente*, they constitute a cook-shop, and are the general diet of the lower orders, throughout Portugal. In the country parts, it is varied with vegetables.

The Portuguese have, almost all, black hair and black eyes; their dress is much in. the English fashion; but the women wear no bonnets, in lieu of which, a fine veil is thrown over the bead. The men, to make up for this deficiency, wear enormous cocked hats, like what we call opera hats. There are many capital buildings in Lisbon, and the statue of Joseph II. in Black-Horse Square, is reckoned, by good judges, to vie with any in Europe. The offices of the inquisition still remain in Russia Square, and I am credibly informed that all the horrid instruments are still there, for applying the question, torture, &c. The different sorts of torture outstrip the inventions of the savages in America, and the scenes acted here have been as infernal as any we read of. Thank God, our power is, at present, predominant here, and I hope will continue so, while I remain here.

ROMAN WALLS

Lisbon is surrounded with a number of fine gardens, well stocked with orange, lime, lemon, and fig-trees. These gardens arc totally different from an English one, being laid out with large walks, and embroidered with beautiful flowers, though thinly scattered. The orange blossoms emit a delightful scent, in the season. The queen's gardens appear to be the best, and superb beyond anything I could expect. There are few vegetable gardens anywhere.

About Buenos Ayres, all persons of condition reside: it is several hundred feet above the river, of which it comprehends a grand view. You can also see St. Ubes, on the opposite side, where the fine Lisbon salt is made. On that side is a sand-bank not so high as Buenos Ayres; some part is cultivated, but not much. The bank coming so close to the river prevents it from expanding into that picturesque scenery which generally enlivens the banks.—On the top of this bank are a number of mills, as I have already stated. Belem Castle is handsomely situated, projecting into the river; but it is not considered of any strength: there are no cannon on it actually serviceable. The Moorish convent at Belem, St. Francisco, is one of the most beautiful moresque, or Gothic pieces of architecture, I ever beheld. The stone of which it is composed, is yellow—and the ornaments about the grand entrance, which reaches to the top of the building, surpass my powers of description; the door is in perspective. We have made an hospital of part of it, for our sick and wounded, and the monks give their assistance, as, indeed, the vast number of them can be of little use in any other way. The castle of Lisbon appears to be strong; it overlooks the town, but could be of little defence to it, as it stands too much in the centre. It might, indeed, annoy any shipping in the river, but it would overwhelm the houses in the town with the concussion.

The river is about a mile over at Lisbon; but after it passes the city, it widens to four or five miles; where, on a sudden, it separates into many small divisions, one of which runs as far as Madrid, the capital of Spain.

Most of the houses have gilt balconies, from the second story upwards, according to the wealth of the possessors. The common staircases are mostly in a very filthy condition, as one family occupy each floor, with a separate hall to themselves. It confirms an old proverb, that every body's business is nobody's, .for they should agree to keep the staircase clean among them, but none of them do it.

There is a fine Roman aqueduct near the city, which is still in use; it was formerly of much greater length, but the various changes of nature have swept part of it away, as Lisbon has frequently experienced, one of the most awful of human calamities, earthquakes. The last was in 1755, on the 13th of November, when most of the buildings were thrown down, and curious to say, the only one untouched was the Inquisition.

Lisbon stood on the south side of the river, in the time of the Romans; after which, it was removed to where the bed of the river now is. The last overthrow left it as it is at present situated. No appearances of any of these destructions remain, although ships now ride at anchor where this city once stood.

I now had orders to join my regiment, and to my great joy, found the 20th regiment had arrived, two days before me, from Corunna, having been thirty-three days at sea. They intended to have disembarked at Corunna; but in consequence of Lord Wellington's retreat from Burgos, they concluded it would be unsafe, and embarked again for Lisbon. Here I met my old friend, Gordon, and as we did not seem willing to part, we agreed to mess together. I next began drawing rations for myself and servant, one ration being one pound and a half of bread, one pound of meat; one pint of wine; two ounces of rice, for soup; one candle, and fifteen pounds of wood per day.

On the third of December, General Peacock, commanding officer in Lisbon, sent me orders to join the 48th regiment, and to move forward with a detachment of it to join the army. Here I took leave of Gordon, with whom I left my extract book, in my own hand-writing, as a keepsake, and he gave me, in return, a dictionary of foreign words, as a remembrance. Marshal Beresford refused to do anything for Read, and the poor fellow was obliged to return to Ireland.

Having too much baggage, I was forced to buy a small trunk, and leave a number of things behind me. I should have sold them, but an assistant-surgeon of one of the regiments advised me to leave them, and I have never seen anything of them since.

I had many billets in Lisbon, but could not well investigate their manners in so short a time. At my last billet, the people were very civil, and often asked me to sup with them; but I declined doing so, as their language was unknown to me. The gentleman of the house would address me in French, of which I understood a little, and when he was absent, signs were resorted to as the mode of converse. This method being unpleasant, I kept clear of it as much as possible, although their good nature often prevented me.

The convents in Lisbon are very spacious, and frequently on a wet day, a regiment or two was reviewed in one of the aisles, which was sufficiently large for doing so.

I found the Portuguese very fond of church music, as our ears were incessantly bored with their bells. In some places where they have bells, no steeples appear; but we find places built no higher than houses, with merely two walls and a roof to support the bells. When they pull the clappers, they do not move the bells, which are in general very large. This is a regale to the people of Lisbon, and the bells are jingled as fast as the players can make a tintamat from morning till night. We found fruit very dear here, but, in general, all commodities were much on a par, in point of price, with England.

December 4.—Having, the evening before, acquainted the people where I was billeted that I was to leave Lisbon next morning, they wished me good night, and left the doors so as I could shut them after me. Next morning (4th) I arose as I thought about five, and quitted the house for Belem, but in passing by the church of St. Roche, I heard it strike four: here

The Tagus near Thomar

I found a coffee-house, hard by, open; I broke my fast, and found it of service to me afterwards.

On my arrival at Belem, I found the troops occupying the flat-bottomed boats, and as I was about to step in, one of the soldiers, but who I could never learn, asked me and another, if we had not blankets with us. As we did not immediately comprehend this, he started off, and brought us from the stores, a pair each, of beautiful ones, which proved to be of material benefit, and we should have been much at a loss without them.

Our detachment consisted of Captain Bricknell, 24th; Captain Parsonage, 53rd; Lieutenants Hunter, De Lacy, and Clarke, 48th; Ensigns Crow, Hambley, and Parsons, 48th; and about two hundred men, 48th; Oliver for the 88th, and myself, with my own detachment, 48th. We were in five boats; set sail about eight o'clock, and bid *adieu* to Lisbon.

In this day's voyage up the river, we had a glorious feast for our eyes, as the scenery, after passing Lisbon, enlarges, and there are no considerable hills to intercept the view. The shore is agreeably interspersed with groves of orange-trees, limes, and olives, and the river widens to four or five miles; but the channel is consequently shallower, and we often ran aground, our boats being deep in the water, as they were full of men. The day was rather dull, from no sun appearing, and the cold off the water made us all very chilly, except the rowers. We were obliged to sit still, hemmed in as we were for want of room. This day we passed the end of the lines made by Lord Wellington; they extended many miles, as far as Cintra, on the seashore, so as completely to shut up Lisbon. We saw them stretching along the top of a range of hills; they certainly were the strongest field-works I ever beheld. There was not only a very deep ditch, but in many places two or three, according to the strength of the approach: the inner entrenchment was defended, at intervals, by strong batteries, and a string of embrasures ran along the whole line. This answered the purpose of changing the cannon, when circumstances required it; and when not wanted for cannon, the infantry made use of them for a surer mark. These approaches were well staked with sharpened poles, pointing outwards, and the glacis for musket-shot distance was perfectly level, and no hills commanded the post from without. Such were the lines of Cintra.

We arrived about four o'clock at Villa Franca, twenty-two miles by water, and thirty by land. We had often run aground, as we kept near shore, and the tide was out. Our boats were so heavy, that when once aground, it required great ingenuity and trouble to get them clear again: at one time we were all stuck in the mud together. From the river our gun-boats annoyed the French left wing very much, when Lord Wellington defended himself behind his works. We were, of course, masters of the river at all times, and this was of material prejudice to the French, and proved a defence to the wing of our own line.

On our arrival at Villa Franca, we were nettled to find it such a wretched place. The houses had no glass in the windows, and the frames or shutters were often wanting. None of the doors were painted, and we went to bed, heartily tired, and slept, in hopes of discovering something tomorrow more agreeable. We dined on sorry beef-steaks and bad bread, with sour wine, and slept on flock beds.

Dec, 5.—This morning, when our detachment had assembled, we were about beginning our march, when a difficulty arose how we were to get our baggage transported. The case was simply this: if we could not purchase mules or asses, we must even carry bag and baggage ourselves. There was no great store of money between us all: however, after running about for an hour, Parsonage, Oliver, Bricknell, and I, contrived to buy an ass to carry our baggage. The rest clubbed in the same way. At last we moved forward, having picked out a servant named Bell. We were that night to halt at a little village called Azambuja, distant sixteen miles. The road to this place was very bad. We passed a poor desolate village, named Villa Nova, or the New Village; but to me it seemed an old one, as few of the houses were standing. The country did not appear very mountainous; the land seemed to contain a good soil, but the Portuguese cultivate it but very little. From the heat of the climate it has taken a reddish hue. There is no want of wood, which contributes to diversify the scenery. The trees are in clusters, but without any regularity. On our march to Azambuja, we stopped to drink our king's health in a well of fine water, of which there are many on the roads, a blessing highly prized in a warm climate.

On our approach to the town, which is nearly in ruins, we were surprised at seeing a few fields (the only ones we saw) completely overran with mushrooms. Of these we collected great numbers, but on shewing them to the people where we were billeted, they begged us not to eat them, as they were poisonous. I was willing to comply, but our mess determined to have them stewed in their soup, and they made as excellent a dish as ever I tasted, to the surprise of the inhabitants, who had never known that they were eatable. Perhaps from this circumstance they may become great mushroom eaters. There is no where a greater plenty of them. After dinner we were regaled with plenty of lime-juice punch, a very agreeable beverage. We had good beds, and slept soundly, but with our feet blistered, not being used to walk so much, and from having been so long cooped up on board ship.

Dec. 6.—To Santarem the distance is about fourteen miles. The road today is much better than yesterday's, and we had abundance of water on the road. We passed a small village on the Tagus, Cartaxo, which had been Lord Wellington's headquarters twice. The church was nearly in ruins, as indeed were almost all the small towns about here, before we came. The landscapes are magnificent, varying and winding along the banks of the river. The opposite sides are covered with trees, with here and there a rude rock projecting, and forming a pretty rural scene. Oranges were cheap here, in comparison to Lisbon, and now the price of everything began to be reasonable.

Santarem is a fine large town, divided into the upper and lower. There are many convents in this place, occupying about half the town. Many of these we had converted into hospitals for our sick and wounded. One of the convents in the Upper Town was of an immense size and height; on the top was a telegraph to communicate with Villa Franca and Abrantes, both which places were visible from it. This was the medium whereby Lisbon knew every transaction relating to the army, before any dispatches could arrive. This place is as bad as Lisbon for bells; the inhabitants boast of 22 different sets, which at times were all going; a blessed retirement and solace for our sick men.

Outside this place are the remains of some Roman walls, at least worth seeing, were it only for their antiquity. The town is surrounded with orange groves, which are very pleasing: the streets abominably dirty. Having beckoned to Parsons to join company, he made one dash forward across the street, when be sunk up to the knees in mud. Major Royal, who commanded here, very politely invited us to dinner on the 7th, the day we halted. The view was extensive from the telegraph, but the day was gloomy.

On the 8th we proceeded to Gallagao, fourteen miles, and on the 9th to Punhete, twelve miles. The road to this place was excellent; we passed many fine groves of olives, and about half way descended into a large glen, where the thick foliage of the trees almost shut out the day. We were obliged to ascend again, and after some difficulty scaled the top, which was very rugged. Having gone on about a hundred yards, we came to a turning in the road, where a view opened transcendently beautiful. Having turned the angle, we came to a small bridge over a stream flowing into the Tagus. In front of us was the Tagus, which here. expanded into a large lake. In the centre was a green island, strewed with the venerable ruins of a Moorish palace, of which we could distinguish the towers in several places remaining. It extended over a very large space. On the whole we were much entertained with our walk. The road wound round the lake to the opposite side, about two miles, and was as smooth as fine sand could make it. On all sides appeared a diversity of woods projecting here and there, and to close and enliven the back scene, a beautiful village, most of the people of which were fishermen. This afforded the handsomest scene we had witnessed since we left Lisbon. Punhete is a very dirty town, the houses very poor, the inhabitants miserably so; but the town itself is romantically situated at the foot of two long hills by the side of a river. The buildings rise to the top of the hill, on which there is a chapel, where our troops were quartered. The streets are very steep, and most of them have steps to them. The houses in general of the towns hereabouts are without paint or glass, the shutters being open in the daytime.

Dec, 10.—To Abrantes, the distance is ten miles. A tolerably good road, but the last mile up to the town dreadfully fatiguing. There are two roads leading to it, one winding along the Tagus, and the other through the valleys and woods, both about the same distance. The town is situated at the top of the highest mountain in this part of the country; it is defended with a very strong castle and outworks. The castle is furnished, as well as the outworks, with many pieces of heavy cannon and mortars. It presents a panorama of all the country round, in every direction, to the edge of the horizon. It also defends the town, which it overlooks, and we were of opinion that a few soldiers might defend it against an army.

They have cut away a great part of the rock inside the castle, to level it, leaving, however, the highest part in a square, for a telegraph, which communicates between Castel Branco and Santarem. The fortifications are irregular; there seemed to have been formerly three bastions projecting at the town side of the castle, but they are now in disuse. The town is both dirty and ugly, in every respect. There are a few good houses In it, but they only serve to ridicule the rest, which are mere pig-styes, swarming with vermin, and loaded with all kinds of filth, We drew rations here, and halted till the 13th, when we had orders to march back to Punhete, and thence to take another route northwards.

14th.—Punhete already described.

15th.—To Thomar, twelve miles, up and down mountains almost all the way. The road very bad, so that artillery could never scale the heights. Indeed, I cannot but wonder how any four, or even two-wheeled carriages can move along many of the Portuguese roads. As mules and asses are the general mode of conveyance in the country, their roads, as it may be expected, are extremely wretched. The scenery was very woody, principally fir, but the road so intricate as to render guides necessary.

As we approached Thomar it appeared a delightful place, pleasantly situated in a plain, at the foot of a hill. It is not very large, but the streets are wide and clean, and the houses well built and neat, with gilt balconies to most of them, as in Lisbon. Here is a manufactory for webs, stockings, &c. which, luckily for the owners, the French never injured, having levied a contribution on it to the amount of fifty thousand new crowns (two shillings and sixpence each.) This manufactory is at one side of a very old bridge, reported, by common fame, to have been built by Hannibal, originally. There is an excellent market-house here; all the houses are built of stone, and roofed with tile, which is the general mode of building throughout Portugal. They commonly use brick in turning arches. They will frequently dash the outside of their houses with plaster, but in general the door and window cases are of cut stone. None of the streets are paved, and this renders walking unpleasant.

On the top of the hill, over the town, is a remarkably fine convent, of prodigious extent; there is only one road up to it, winding round the rocks. In this convent we billeted our men, and were assured by the people that the French had 60,000 infantry, 80 pieces of cannon, and 9000 cavalry, all accommodated at once in it, including even horses and baggage. You enter from the only portal or gateway it has, at the east end of it. When you are in the court-yard, round which are store-houses, stabling, &c. from the four corners, you may ascend as many flights of stairs. I should, however, have mentioned, that round the first court it is all *piazza*, which, in wet weather, affords a protection from the rain. On ascending the stairs, at the corners, you mount to another court-yard, *piazza'd* all round with handsome pillars, with orange-trees and flowers in the centre, like a little garden. Round these gardens are the apartments occupied by the monks, but which were given up to the soldiers, not only this square, but above fifty others. At every landing, is one of these gardens from each of the four corners.

At the top of the building is a chapel, and the abbot's apartments filling up one of those squares. All the monks who had not deserted the convent, had their apartments at the top. We were obliged to place a sentinel at one of the avenues, by desire of the abbot, to prevent intrusion. One of the monks conducted me through every part of it. The chapel is beautifully painted, although the French had taken some of their best pictures away. We could see the places which they had occupied. The chapel was shaped in an octagonal form, each octagon being a little chapel dedicated to some saint. It was pleasantly carpeted, and very warm. I saw also different apartments, wherein they had secret doors to convey anything in or out of a room, without seeing or being seen. The chapel was for the monks only, but the common one for the villagers had been converted into a stable by the French, and an immense capability for the purpose it certainly exhibited. The apartments occupied by the monks were very neat and clean, but the length and number of the galleries surprised me beyond measure.

The French had carried away everything worth taking; but the remains of many places might well tempt an epicure to turn monk, to enjoy such luxuries as had been there, and doubtless were there still, though concealed. The Portuguese had, by this time, lost enough, from their rarity of exposing to the French the riches of their country. Of this wealth they had been often deprived; and here I might ask, why should so many thousands live on the fat of the land, and so idly? Some of the galleries extended to the length of three hundred paces, and a great many to two hundred. There were so many windings in this labyrinth, this convent of romance, that had I not been assisted by a guide, I should have lost myself.

Thomar is the handsomest place I have seen in Portugal. Captain Bricknel, who commanded the detachment, was bent on having a grand house to be billeted in, and he pointed out one himself to the mayor, adorned with gilt balconies, and to all appearance a noble mansion. The mayor was obliged to comply, and B. went to the house, but it had never been finished, and none of the floors were laid. This afforded us much merriment for some time after, as B. was one of the most good-humoured characters I was ever acquainted with.

On the 16th, we moved forward to Farreira, distant about twelve miles; but our guide, by mistake, led us to another small town, which made a distance of four or five miles extra. This day's march fatigued us very much, as, in recovering our way, we were obliged to leave the road, and scale some lofty hills, covered with fern and wild thyme. After leaving Punhete, we had to traverse a mountainous district, though in' a few places there were some cultivated plots of ground between the hills. The olive-trees are torn up, and Indian corn sown in lieu of them. Some places show wheat, but most of the Portuguese live on what they call "*Milho Pao*," which means flour bread, but is, in fact, Indian corn ground fine. It is as yellow as saffron, and when made into bread, they must be very careful in baking it, as no water will make it stick well together, it is of such a dry nature. If eaten when fresh, you must break it off short, or it will crumble to pieces. It is uncommonly sweet, but not disagreeable; eating more like a saffron cake than anything I can compare it to.

Farreira is a poor place, but there was a capital nobleman's seat here, in which we were billeted. On going into one of the rooms, we observed a bier, and on questioning the person who kept the *chateau*, or *quinta*, she said a person had died there, but was buried the day before. We afterwards found the body, which had not been buried, but lay hid in a closet, und the waking was postponed till after our departure. We thought we smelt the body, when told that it had been in the house, and one of the servants had seen it. Here was room for exploring what could be the reason of concealing it from us, who would have done them no injury. The fact is this: had we seen it, and any of us touched it, the dead person must have gone to purgatory, in consequence of being defiled by the touch of a heretic. So much for the pious delusions of Catholic superstition!

We found this house beautifully fitted up; it was tolerably large, and had every convenience attached to it. A most excellent library was still remaining, little injured from the accidents of war. Some few valuable books only were missing, as everyone took what they liked. We found in one of the rooms, which seemed to have been a store-room, several barrels of dried fruits, apples, peaches, grapes, and prunes, of which last we ate a great quantity, being better preserved than any of the others. It proved as potent as a dose of *jalap*, in opening our bowels, for several days after. The men, too, had plenty of them from our servants.

We were total strangers to the effects of such fruit. The gardens were beautifully laid out, but overrun with weeds. There were some beehives in the garden, one of which one of our soldiers plundered, for which he was punished, as the person who had charge of the house permitted us every liberty, but wished us not to injure the hives, which seemed to be the only thing they took any care of. The window shutters of this house were stuck full of musket balls, a party of the French having been in it, but driven out by our troops. The floors were all stained with blood, which could not be got out by any means.

Dec. 17.—To Cabecoa twelve miles

18th.—To Chou de Cocae ten miles—the people wretched, dirty, and half-starved; the roads bad, and the streets preferable to the houses to sleep in.

19th.—To Espanheil, a handsome looking town, but dirty. The Portuguese in general are poor and dirty: the Irish are clean in comparison. We drew six days' rations here. The church is well adapted for a Portuguese congregation, as it is filthy enough.

20th.—Halted, much fatigued both in body and mind.

21st. —To Miranda de Corvo, a very fine road, the scenery rural, and the country well cultivated. The peasants were pruning their vines, and I heartily wished the vintage in.

The grape-tree, or vine, grows like a gooseberry or currant bush, two or three feet high, and about three yards asunder; they are planted in rows. The peasants, in pruning them, cut off all the branches, leaving only the stump, with the remains of the branch, about half an inch in length. These shoot out again, and in the vintage, will be ten or twelve feet long; the best grapes grow about the stump, which you cannot see for fruit. The people here were very civil, and gave us freely a share of what they had. From this town we had a grand, distinct view of some very lofty mountains, at an immense distance.

The country was very mountainous in our approaches to Miranda, which is pleasantly situated on a large river. There are two churches; one of them was converted into temporary barracks. As we strolled round this place, we observed a funeral of a child, and followed it to the church. When brought in, it was gently laid on the floor. The corpse was superbly decorated with ribbons. We observed that the four old women that brought it, kneeled down. The priest who attended did not kneel, nor his attendants; one of them held the holy water, another the crucifix, and the third a lighted wax candle; although it was three in the day, and the sun almost vertical. The priest said a few prayers standing, then sprinkled the child with the holy water, without any apparent concern.

This mummery lasted about three minutes, and then the priest retired with his, attendants. Another man, the sexton, I presume, pulled up a board of the floor in the chapel, and presently dug a hole, perhaps eighteen inches deep, but not more than two feet, and then put the child in, without a coffin. While he was digging the grave, the women were busily employed in stripping the child of its finery, which they took away with them, leaving the body with only a loose wrapper on. When it was put in, the man threw the earth in, walking on it to press it down, and alternately beating it to make the board fit, as it did before the body was placed there. After all, the grave-digger could not manage the point, with all his skill, and was obliged to carry out some of the mould to the outside, to his no small vexation. The trouble which it cost him to carry a shovel full or two, about twenty yards, disgusted us, though we were almost inclined to laugh at his laziness.

Dec. 22—To St. Miguel de Poyares ten miles; the road very intricate, winding through a vast variety of high hills, well wooded with fir. From some places we had a distant view of the heights of Busaco, from which Lord Wellington had been forced to retreat, by the French outflanking out line last year. The position was very strong, and the scenery romantic. The heights were lofty, and superbly grand, as they rose bold and abrupt. The country hereabouts is slightly cultivated, but the village is poor. The church seemed to be very respectable.

Dec. 23.—To Sobrina and St. Martini, two petty villages, twelve miles. Our detachment was hard put to it to get lodgings in the two. Sobrina is the best, but St. Martini has a church. The road to this place is tolerably good, winding near the heights of Busaco, which rise towering above our heads. We crossed the Alva, (a river often dyed with blood in the course of this war) by a small bridge which had been blown up, but since repaired with wood, as well as even All the bridges I have seen in Portugal appear to have been injured in the same way.

Dec. 24.—To Villa da Valha twelve miles; a miserable place, so much so, that we were forced to go forward to another village, called Esparis, two miles further. Our feet by this time were much cut up, by walking continually in a warm climate, over a soil which is worse than hard rocks, as the sand gets into your shoes, and grinds your feet to pieces. However, we limped to it, and found better accommodation here than at Villa Valha. I had a most excellent billet, as the people shared everything with us. Fine wine and oranges were in the greatest perfection, and we rested ourselves, to our satisfaction, after a hard day's march.

We had met on the road, which is tolerably good, the skeleton of a man whom we supposed to have belonged to the 27th regiment. He appeared to have been murdered, for some of his clothing lay scattered about, and the dogs and birds had picked off the flesh of all parts, except the legs, which were only half gone. The arms were gone entirely. The teeth were perfect, mod those of a young man. Why the country people would not fake the trouble of burying him gave us some concern, at there was a village at a hundred yards distance. I lamented his fate, as we all did: perhaps he bad affectionate friends in England, a wife, a sister, or a mother, anxiously waiting to hear of his welfare. We buried him, however, and it was the general belief that he had been some sick soldier on his way to a depôt, who had fallen into chat with some of the Portuguese, who seeing him defenceless, set on him, and murdered him, on the score of religion. The like had often happened to some of our men. This village was a tolerably good one, with some decent mud-houses in it, which, bad as they were, proved to be more than usually convenient.

Dec. 25.—To Galizes, ten miles, Christmas day, a delightful road, but from its raining incessantly, we were as cold as I ever felt a December month in Ireland. The road is one of the best in Portugal; on the sides are woods of fir, abounding with wolves. We saw some examples of these destroying whatever was eatable that came in their way. Many of the woods we found deeply cut into by the different armies which had encamped on the road side. The first thing the men do is to cut down the trees about four feet from the root, for firing, and stretching their blankets, at night, on the tops of these, the soldiers lie tolerably free from the heavy dews, which often fall among the woods. The scenery of this day's march I must reserve for a future delineation, as I could not see a hundred yards before me, we were so enveloped with the heavy fogs. No accommodation was to be had in Galizes, so we were ordered forward to Villa Poco, where we were accommodated, partly in a village, and partly in a large convent. Here we spent Christmas day, amidst a group of forests, convents, mountains, rivers, wolves, &c. The cold here was intense, with a troublesome drizzling rain, more penetrating than a heavy shower. We dined on wretched soup, made of beef as tough as leather, nor would any boiling make it tenderer. We procured, however, a small allowance of rum, which partly served to keep the cold out.

Dec. 26.—We now set off for Torrasillas, a delightful road, distance fourteen miles. Here we fell in with a cluster of mountains, called Sierra de Estrella, which are reported to stretch as far as to the Pyrenean mountains. To comprehend our road, imagine three long hills, or rather the middle one a hill, and those at the sides tremendous mountains between us and them: let fancy mark deep valleys, well cultivated, the tops of the mountains all level, and on the top of the middle or lowest mountain, our road, winding over a level. The mountains on each side were at least ten miles from us, but their amazing height, particularly to the right, made them appear within a stone's throw.

Those to the right were twice as high as those on the left; and in the highest part of this right hand range, which accompanied us, as it were, many days, there was an immense cavity in the side, not unlike a shelf, on which we saw a very large village about half way up the mountain. The road up to it seemed to us almost perpendicular. We had not sufficient

A Day's Attack in the Mountains Sierra de Estrella

time, or we should have visited it, if possible, although our feet had suffered so much from fatigue, that we all longed for a day's halt, to rest.

In these valleys appear not a few villages, but all black and dirty, which, with the dark green forests, rocky mountains, now entirely capped with snow, and raising their awful forms to such a stupendous height, impressed a picture on my fancy which will not easily be erased

As we approached Torrasillas, the country began to look greener, because better cultivated. It was full of military parties. We put our men into an old chapel, and went ourselves to a small village, called Villa Doce, which was much cleaner than Torrasillas. Here we had good billets and beds, and the people were very civil.

Dec. 27th.—To Cea, the day freezing cold, nine miles. We could not get billets here; the town was full of our men, it being the headquarters of the 6th division. We were obliged to go forward to Penhances, a small village about two miles further. Cea is a considerable town, and may easily be distinguished by a large convent, which is higher on the hill than the town, and first attracts the eye. This convent is nearly in ruins; only a part being inhabited by a few old nuns—certainly no great objects of admiration. These were the first nuns I had, as yet, seen in Portugal.

Our road this day wound along the side of the Sierra de Estrella, which probably might occasion the intense cold. The scenery was much the same as the last day's route, except our meeting with a vast number of dead bullocks lying by the road side, a sure indication of our drawing near to the army. When we left Cea, we had to descend, for some time, till we came to a river, over which we passed by a small bridge; then we again mounted up a large hill from the bridge. The mountain atone side came very bold forwards, with projecting masses of rock, which seemed as if they were about leaving their hold; to come rolling' down the mountain. Penhances is a place not worth description, lying amongst enormous rocks.

In this day's march, we lost our way, but having, at last, obtained a guide, we moved forward and came to a river, over which there was no bridge, as it was only knee deep. At one place, those who could jump well, might cross. Most of the detachment got over here. Some not acquitting themselves with activity, were repaid by falling in, and as the place was narrow, the water was deeper, and they had a sound ducking. While all was anxiety, Captain Bricknell seated himself on a stone near where the water was broadest, and not deep; he then pulled out a luncheon of bread and an onion, and began eating. After this he began singing—

> I am not such a fool
> That I need go to school;
> But I know a sheep's head from a carrot, a carrot;

which he repeated several times, to our infinite merriment; and when we were all over, he pulled off his shoes and stockings, raised his trowsers, and walked through to us. He then wiped and redressed his feet: we laughed, but he told us we were on the wrong side of the joke, for this bathing would refresh and cure his feet from blisters, which it certainly did, while ours were dreadfully lacerated and burnt.

We thought this day's march would never end, although a small one. On asking a Portuguese how many leagues it was to Cea, he would reply, two very big leagues "*deux legues grandes;*" the next, after walking a mile or two, would say, two leagues, not very big; the third, two leagues (*piquenos*) or little; the next, two leagues, and so on. And, verily, we thought the Legues *piquenos* and *grandes*, would never end—they are so large. Our patience having often been, in a manner, exhausted, when we were much tired in this way, some of us would swear at the poor Portuguese, who answered us according to truth, with politeness. They would then turn with a shrug or a sneer from us. I saw, at Cea, the 42nd Highland regiment, in their kilts, and was at a loss to think how they could bear the cold as they did; but they did not seem to mind it.

Dec. 28th.—To Villa de Cortez, nine miles. Here again, we met a vast number of dead bullocks on the road. This town is still on the side of the Sierra de Estrella, which is nearly even all along, and the same at the top, but of an astonishing height. The village is poor, but governed, as all the smallest or larger ones are, by a Juis de Fora, or a magistrate, answering the same purpose as ours. The larger towns have generally a *capitan* mayor, who commands a district, and holds correspondence with the government.

We are now about the centre of the army, having passed some of the cavalry at Esparis. The country looks barren, nothing hardly to be seen but rocky cliffs lifting their sublime crests even above the clouds. Only here and there a few trees or woods appear; but we must remember that it is now winter. The valleys seem to be well cultivated in the summer time, when it must be a charming country. There are a few villages scattered about, thinly, just enough to give some idea of habitations, and the haunts of men.

Dec. 29th.—To Celerico, nine miles, the roads still the same, perfectly even, and along the Sierra. On our arrival at Celerico, we found it an hospital for our sick, among whom the mortality was dreadful, sixteen or seventeen dying in a day: there were six hundred sick here at this time. This place stands on a hill, separate from any other—it had been formerly a handsome town, and now has many good houses in it. The highest part is surmounted by the remains of one of those ancient Moorish castles, still visible, but of this there is little left. It stood on a pile of rocks hanging over the town, and was originally built in an hexagonal form, but only three sides now remain. In the centre of it is a very large tower, which probably was the citadel; it is very high, and commands the town.

The whole is in ruins, except the shell; the walls are about ten feet thick, but without embrasures. The top of the wall is perfectly flat, with steps up to it, the same as what I have often observed in our modern fortifications. When on the top, you may walk entirely round on the wall. At present, we cannot exactly say what its former strength might have been, but it was evidently situated on an almost inaccessible point of rocks. Not being accommodated at Celerico, we moved forward to a small village, Espanharia, two miles further on, among the cliffs and rocks. In our march to this place, we had to cross a bridge which had been very much battered by our cannon, as we were informed.

January 1st,—To Faaens, about eight miles, over the Sierra de Estrella, but away from the main road. This day's route would be only passable for infantry; it is on the top of a mountain full of rocks, and, on the left hand, a tremendous precipice frightful even to look down. The mountains, this day, were beginning to be stored with different sweet herbs, wild thyme, rosemary, lemontine, and the wild rose, all which diffused a fragrant odour. The day was foggy, or we should have had some delightful views. The man on whom I was billeted was surly, and the people of this town, seemed to have, a dislike to us all: I will not pretend to account for this. The town was tolerably clean and neat.

January 2nd.—To Moreira, eight miles, a very fair road. We here begin to leave the Sierra de Estrella, and lose sight of snowy cliffs. The road to this place passes over a very high mountain, from which the prospect is unbounded over the whole country. Here we appeared so elevated above the world below, that we were, in a manner, lost to it. Here and there some bold mountains would penetrate the mass of clouds at our feet, and raise their aspiring heads above us. The morning dew and mists of the valley had not yet disappeared, and lay rolling in volumes, like the sea, below us.

The sun shining bright gave it a novel appearance, till we became familiarized to it. These clouds were several hundred feet below us, and we had again another tier of lighter clouds above us, not thick or gross, but such as there are on a very fine day. The mountains which penetrated through these lower tiers, were like so many islands which they resembled, in a sort of sea-scene, being only more abrupt. About four miles on our road, we came to a fine town, Trancoso, once fortified, but now, with many parts of the walls, in ruins. This place appears to have been defended in the Roman manner, or, at least, of very ancient date. It has many square towers, and a wall going round the town, with a successive communication between the towers. The wall is about sixteen feet high, and the towers overtop the walls about eight feet, except at the gateway or entrance, where that tower is double, and as high again as the wall.

The whole fortification forms an exact square. On the east side is the citadel adjoining the wall: it is a curious specimen of the ancient mode of fortification. The town must have been very handsome, in its pristine glory, but now 'tis dreadfully dirty. On your entrance into it, you come into a street which has the front of all the houses projecting in a continued *piazza*, under which you walk. It is full of shops, not unlike our Haymarket theatre arcade, but far inferior to it in point of beauty. It is, however, of the same form and manner, and possesses the advantage of being real cut stone. There are many fine churches in the town; but we had no time to stop and examine their interior.

Moreira, like other towns here, is situated on the top of a very high mountain, from which the prospect reaches to Almeida, to Pinhel, to the frontiers of Spain and Portugal, Ciudad Rodrigo, &c. It is a very neat town, beautifully situated, and we found the people very civil. My host presented me with a great quantity of fine grapes, as fresh as just pulled; these lie had preserved since the vintage. I took them, and went out to a large rock, where I sat down to indulge my genius in the treat. I had a glass in my hand to view the country, which exhibited an immense panorama.

The sun shone bright; it was warm, and not a breath of air

RUINS OF A MOORISH CASTLE NEAR MOREIRA

NATURAL ROCKS

stirring, or the least noise. Everything was hushed and tranquil, as if I were the only inhabitant on the globe. At my feet lay the dwellings of once busy men, whose toils now seemed over. This was a pleasure at once intellectual and sensitive; my mind returned to my friends, and memory, that sometimes sleeps, awakes at such moments of gay recreation, to recall past scenes. No words can adequately express my feelings while brooding over this expanse.

Moreira has two churches; at the outside of one of them, they have hollows cut in the level rocks, exactly the shape of the human body, to correspond with coffins. Those that are occupied, are filled with sods for a lid, but most of them are empty. The singularity of the matter excited our curiosity very much; perhaps it may explain to naturalists, the petrifaction of bodies found in stone, as, in a long lapse of years, the stone may grow over the body. One thing seemed curious to us, that there was not a loose body or bone to be found about the churchyard.

Moreira is built entirely among rocks. One of these is 57 feet round, and 20 feet high; the bottom flat and only resting on two feet of rock, like a mushroom. We had passed hundreds of these rocks, within the last few days, sticking on a single point, and very few on more. These rocks will incline with the ground, and we have frequently pushed against one, on the side of a mountain, thinking to shove it down a precipice, but all our labour was in vain. Many of them would, I imagine, weigh one hundred tons. The mountains, for the last few days, resemble very much the fabulous accounts of Ossa and Pelion, where the giants fought with the gods: for the rocks seem as if they had been hurled to and fro, in their many curious situations, effected, probably, by some dreadful convulsion of nature. As we leave the mountains, the country, in general, becomes batter cultivated.

Outside of Moreira are the remains of a small Moorish tower. It is built on the top of several rocks, piled one on the other. The situation might have been good in ancient warfare, but now that artillery is in use, it can hardly be called a fortress. Indeed, an enemy at the foot could never take it; but it is commanded by three or four hills, at 100 yards distance. The walls are ten feet thick, and the view I have taken presents the only remains of it, the inside being a ruinous aggregate of pieces of massy walls and columns.

January 3rd.—To Villosa, eight miles, a very pleasant walk. The town is a good one, but poor. The house where I was billeted was respectable, and the inhabitants rich. When I found the house, the *patron*, as the master is always termed in Portugal, kept me a long time at the door, previous to being admitted. I could hear the people inside removing their furniture to a cellar underneath, to secrete it from us, as if we were a gang of thieves. At last, being let in, I found the house almost empty, and seeing a basket of grapes, I made free to take some, after due permission, as they are not counted of much value here; but to me they were an excellent repast.

January 4th.—To Meda, where we joined the 48th regiment, and ended our long march of one month's duration, with some few days of rest. We were on foot all the way, no allowance being made for horses; and not being much accustomed to walking, I, at first, suffered severely; but after a week's continued route, was much better able to bear it. The weather had been variable, to an extraordinary degree—some days being at cold and wet as a severe winter's day in Ireland; and others at fine and warm as we must expect in a hot climate. The fact is, that one part of our march lay among tremendous mountains, which are sure to attract any damp cloud that comes near them, and keep it there, until it falls from continued accumulation.

The country was, in several places, well cultivated; but a general indolence seemed to pervade every class of the lower orders. The soil was not half cultivated, and the woods were very thick all over the country, serving as a receptacle for wolves, of which we could see many, during the hard weather, prowling about the dead bullocks in the road. For such a short period as we stopped in each village, I had little opportunity of examining particulars minutely; and our continued fatigue helped to damp our curiosity, as rest was requisite to prepare for another day's march.

At Celerico, we parted with Brickell, Hunter, Parsonage, and Oliver. The ass that carried our baggage was to separate from some of us here; the case was rather an awkward one, as none of us bad a penny to spare, nor would either lose his part of the property. However, Parsonage met a brother officer at Celerico, who lent him some money to repay us, and Delacey allowed me room on his mule to carry my baggage.

Meda is a large town with many fine houses. At one end of it, there is a curious accumulation of rocks which rise about a hundred feet, piled one on the other. On this, there was usually planted a sentinel as a look out. The day I joined the regiment, I was invited to dine with our major, White, (now lieutenant-colonel) and so on in regular rotation, round the whole party of officers on one side of the town. Here we observed some cork-trees, not less than thirty feet round; they don't grow very high, but are of an immense bulk. On the branches grows a species of moss, which is generally used as tinder, after being dried in the sun.

I went to two balls here, given by Colonel Wilson and Major White; there was nothing but dancing and cold sweetmeats, without any supper; this is the usual mode in Portugal. The Portuguese dance uncommonly slow, but the figure is curious, the arms and bodies twine round each other, in an intricate manner, and not easily to be caught at first.

Our regiment being distributed into three villages, we were invited by the mess of Posto de Cantes, to go over to dinner there one day; copious libations to Bacchus. I went to see Captain Thwaites home, and De Lacy. When I left them, I walked about a little, it being a fine moonlight night. On coming to the church, who should I see but De Lacy, walking with a cool composure! The night was frosty; he had only his trowsers and shoes on, his coat under his arm, and to all appearance he seemed perfectly comfortable. I inquired what made him leave his bed. He could not stop in it, it seems, for the cold. I got him home, and found he had started, in despite of his servant, to go and warm himself where we all used to walk in the daytime, it being a fine promenade. The Portuguese wines made him mistake the moon for the sun. Next morning, as I was on my return, my horse had to mount a steep hill, and the girths not being properly secured, the saddle slipped over the tail, and down I came, nor stopped till I had rolled to the bottom. To my companions it was mirth enough. This frolic, however, produced three duels next day, through quarrelling.

Feb. 10.—We moved forward to a large town called Freisco, which proved inferior in accommodation to the last. Here Hambly brought the soldier to a court-martial, and had him flogged for plundering the beehives at Fereira. Most of us thought this punishment rather severe. Hambly was now ordered home to England, and I obtained leave to accompany him on a visit to the 9th regiment, near Lamego. He was going home by Oporto, which lay in his way, and we set out accordingly.

Feb. 13.—To Meda, where we spent a pleasant day with Buckley, the Surgeon of our regiment, and formerly assistant-surgeon in the 9th; be gave us several recommendations to the officers of that regiment.

14.—To Cushero eight miles, a dreadful road among frightful rocks and precipices. A poor village. We passed Pennadona, where we saw an old Moorish castle, now used as a gaol.

15.—To Baldos nine miles. We passed a fine village called Rhuadades. On the 16th to Salzedas, where we found the 9th. We stopped and slept with Thornhill, the adjutant, and dined or breakfasted severally, with Captains Percival and Purcell. On the 18th we had a card party, at Lieutenant Harrison's, and I won six dollars. I went to see Lamego, and to get a treat of some bottles of porter, but we were disappointed, as we could find none. This is a large and pretty well built place, but dirty. As usual, there is an old Moorish castle in it in ruins. I saw every fine building here, but had no time to ask what it was. The architecture was elegant and beautiful.

After spending from the 16th to the 19th with the 9th, I left them, with sincere regret. It was the pleasantest portion of time I had spent since I left home. I must report the obliging conduct of Colonel Cameron in terms of gratitude. The union that cemented the officers of this regiment made them like brothers. And I have never witnessed so much of mutual friendship in any regiment as in the 9th. On the 19th, I reached Baldos again, and Hambly having gone on to Oporto, his servant came under my directions, so that I was not altogether alone.

The old man of the house where I was billeted, was a priest, and I found him a very pleasant companion. We had stopped before in his house, but then he was not over polite. I now found him different, even previous to an accident which placed me in his favour in a supreme degree. Since this time, I have made it a rule, when returning to a town where I had been before, to go to my old lodgings, without applying for a billet, and I have always found a kind welcome, and a becoming share of what the table afforded.

The reason of my old host being partial to me was simply this. He was one day shewing me all his valuables, old gilt rosaries, gilt crosses, &c. &c. when, at last, he pulled out an old silver watch, which he said had been out of repair two and twenty years. It was very clean, and his keeping it in a case preserved the works from rusting. On my looking at it, I found it did not go, and, though I know as little of a watch as any other individual, I took off the cap of the verge, and discovered, by a shake, that the verge did not lie in the right place. I reinstated it, and so replaced the cap, as the works were perfectly sound. In short, I wound it up, and it went as well as ever. But who can express the raptures of the poor priest? He danced for joy, and protested, in the fullness of his heart, that he never could spare money enough to have it mended, for he was not, I fancy, of high rank in the priesthood.

On the 20th, I reached Rhuadades

21st.—Cushero.

22nd.—Meda, and stopped with Lieutenant Bulkeley.

23rd.—Freix, where I joined my regiment.

On my arrival, I found letters for me from M——, with fair offers; and, procuring the consent of Major White, I accepted the offers made me of a situation in the commissariat. After bidding *adieu* to the 48th regiment, first purchasing a pony to carry my baggage, and another to ride on, I set out for Coimbra, with my servant in company, a Portuguese, a distance of 150 miles; it was on the 26th of February, 1813.

That day I reached Villosa, sixteen miles distant from where I set out. The weather was quite agreeable, and I went merrily along. The scenery was very good, though with little of cultivation. On the 27th, I reached Moreira, eight miles; on the 28th Espanharia, sixteen miles. March 1st, Villa Cortez, eleven miles; all these places have been noticed. On this day's march, I was to suffer severely, for my servant having complained of fatigue, I let him ride my pony, when he sprang out of my sight, leaving me with the baggage, and I could never learn any more of him. This was a serious inconvenience, as I could get fifty dollars for the pony, and I was dreadfully mauled with having to lead the baggage myself.

My situation now was truly unpleasant. I could speak very little of the language, and being entirely alone, had anything disastrous happened, no account could ever have reached my friends. My spirits sunk; I was alone in a foreign country, and God only knew whether I should ever return to see my friends. It is impossible to paint the agony of my mind during the rest of this day's march. At last, to drown care, I took a draught out of a *calabash* which hung by my side, and smoked

a *segar* along the road. This inspired me with a degree of fortitude; but to define my feelings this day I shall not attempt.

March 2.—I arrived at Penhances, eleven miles. In passing
through a wood, driving my pony before me, I saw several dragoons dismounted, and lying under the shade of some trees
during the heat of the day. As I passed close to them, I asked
if they were going to join their regiments, as they seemed all
of different ones. They told me they were; that they had been
left sick at Celerico, were now convalescent, and were on their
route to Coimbra by easy stages.

I inquired if any of them belonged to the 4th dragoons,
when one man started up, named Noble, and said he did, and
that he was going to join them. I mentioned the circumstance
of my servant running away, when, after a hearty curse, he of-
fered his services to me until we joined the regiment, which
indeed were very acceptable, and the more so, as I had now
one of my own country to talk to. In times like these, very
little ceremony is kept up, the officer very frequently faring
little better than the soldier. The other men made a similar
offer of their services, but I now did not stand in need of them.
However, they all wished to stay by me, and, as they gave me
their route, I became the commanding officer. One drove my
baggage, and as they had their short carbines with them, I bor-
rowed his who was not so well recovered as the rest, and having purchased some powder and shot, amused myself as I went
along, shooting at whatever came in the way—the wolves,
birds, &c.

On the 3rd, we all reached Galizes, a poor place, and here
we drew four days' rations. It was so late when we came in,
that we could not procure billets, and so were obliged to go
into any house we could. The men foraged, somewhere or
other, for themselves, and I went into a house where I heard
a number of English voices. Here I found some of the commissariat, who had arrived late, as well as myself. I asked leave
to stop with them, and it was readily granted. They were not

129

billeted there, however, any more than myself.

There were Mr. Sealy and his lady, Mr. Thompson, now a deputy assistant commissary general, and his lady, a Portuguese, of a horrible temper. Mrs. Sealy behaved very well, and made me a tolerable bed. I went into my room in the dark, and was near foiling through a trapdoor which opened into the stables among the horses; however, I fortunately caught hold of the side before I dropped through. I soon fell asleep, but when a general stillness prevailed, the rats began running over me by dozens, and all my efforts could not drive them away till daybreak. I wounded many, but having no proper weapon, I was unable to kill one. In the morning I breakfasted with Sealy and Thompson, and we agreed, as we were all going the same way, to keep company in each town. Here we drew rations, and I am obliged to denounce the commissariat officer in charge. His wife made him so jealous, that he, in a manner, neglected his duty to watch her. He was very fond of her, though she was of no great account, if common fame may be credited. Sealy quarrelled with him for not giving him rations for two horses. But he was a very indifferent character, Sealy having often assisted him before.

In the morning of the 4th, we set out, but I found some of the men falling off, as they were unable to keep up; and indeed I am apprehensive that we hurt some of them, by making such long marches. Finding they were tired, we halted in a wood, and having lighted a fire, we boiled some eggs, which we had in plenty, and, with some bread and butter, made a comfortable meal. Sealy and his wife joined us, and we shared our luncheon and wine with them. But we were near setting the wood on fire, as the underwood and grass, were as dry as tinder. Had it taken place, it must have run over some miles of ground, as all the fir-trees hereabouts are full of rosin.

We arrived, about three, at Maita, twelve miles; the scenery was cheerful, with a clear sun. We all dined with Thompson, but his wife was peevish, and would not eat. On the 5th, we reached Ponta de Mercella, ten miles. On its river is a ruinous bridge. The place does not show above a dozen houses; Sealy left us here. On the 6th, we reached Foz de Roce, ten miles; a good village, in a pleasant country. The spring just appearing, has embellished the face of nature with a most luxuriant verdure, but we were not able to atop, making forced marches, and many of my men were now behind, Thompson left me here, his road turning in a contrary direction.

March 7—To Coimbra twelve miles. We had a fine view of this place about three miles from it. It is situated on the river Mondago, and rises, with a sort of regular rapidity, on a hill; every house was white-washed. Here are many convents, and an archbishop's palace. Also a college, the most celebrated in. Portugal. One half of the town seems to consist in convents. Most of the buildings are on the northern side of the river. There is a very long bridge over the river, which presents a diversified view of the town, and particularly of a large convent on the south bank, whitewashed also.

This bridge is most curiously raised on two others. The one first built was gradually choked up by the river lodging a quantity of sand against the piers. This increased in time, so as totally to fill up the arches; the river then ran over the bridge. They were, of course, obliged to build another, which, in process of time, became obstructed in like manner. In short, the present bridge is nearly half choked with sand, which increases every year against the arches, and all their endeavours cannot prevent it. There is a Roman aqueduct outside the town, still in good repair, but the stone and cement are quite soft from age. The streets are remarkably steep, the descent of some, dangerous.

The soldier of the 6th Dragoons, who had stuck close to me, came to say that the men who were of the party had been clapped into the black hole, as they arrived, and he feared he should be treated in the same way. I had not adverted to their route, which extended no farther than to this place, and I should have reported myself to Colonel Royal, who had commanded in Santarem, as I passed through. I went to him, however, and told him the circumstance of my meeting them in a wood, and their giving me the route, at which he laughed heartily. As the men, by their own account, had arrived from Celerico, and had no route, their story seemed improbable, and he had them taken up as deserters; but on my representation they were liberated. The man was attached to me the rest of the time, till we joined the 4th dragoons. On the 9th, we went to Santa Martini, seven miles, after drawing rations. Mr. Drake was the commissary.

I was, at one time, in Portugal, shewn into the inside of a nunnery, but all the young nuns were invisible. The confessionals are much like our sentry boxes, with a seat inside, where the monk sits. There is a little wicket window at each side, through which the confession is made, the person being on the outside.

March 10.—To Verride eight miles. I passed a village here, bat have forgot its name; the head-quarters of the first German Heavy Dragoons. Having letters of recommendation to Captain Halpiu, pay-master, I called on him, and the captain wished me to stop a day or two with him, out the urgency of the time would not permit. He also gave me letters to General Bock, who commanded all the cavalry, but I had no occasion for them. The river Mondego, from the town or village, divides into two arms, the ground between them being as flat and level as a table. Outside these arms the country is all overspread with hills. The town itself stands on a hill, like a sugar loaf.

We set out again, and having proceeded about two miles, forded the arm of the river next us, with an intention of pushing forward to the other arm, distant about two miles. As the village we were going to lay on the other side of these arms, we deemed it advisable to cross, before we met with others to pass over. When about a mile across, we met a Portuguese, whose directions we followed, turning to the right for Montemor, where we arrived about four o'clock.

Here we halloed for a long time for a boat, but the people kept us an hour and a half in a state of uneasy suspense. At last I stripped, determined to swim over if I could, expecting, however, to ford most of the way. On reaching the bank, that part on which I stood gave way, and in I plunged, over head and ears. I had never thought myself an expert swimmer, but being now out of my depth, I made a resolve, in about a second, to exert all my strength and fortitude, to extricate myself. The soldier, who had care of my horse and baggage, could not swim, and began to set up a most vehement roar and noise. He loaded his carbine, and fired into the town several times, but the distance, I imagine, was too far. At last, after half an hour's struggling, I reached the other side, and was happy to find myself again on *terra firma*. I felt more gay and lively after this adventure, than at any other period, perhaps, of my life.

Having rested a little, I went to one of the boats, but found it locked by a chain to a tree. This I soon separated, and got into the boat, but there was no oar. At last, I found the withered arm of a tree, and having seized it, ferried myself over as well as I could, being stark naked, towards my man and baggage. But mark, when the mind is ruffled, how common sense and reason escape!

The boat was too small to hold the horse and baggage, and there were larger ones that I might have had, if consideration had taken place. I put on my clothes, therefore, and was about to ferry myself over, when a large boat appeared, manned by some Portuguese, who seeing us near over, through our own exertions, made an offer to convey us all at once. This was done, and we arrived safe on the other side. Before we could reach Verride, we had had five more arms to cross, all of which we got over by ferries. Some we paid for, but as our money was short, we were obliged, in the last two instances, to cross by force, the Portuguese swearing at us for "*diables Inglese.*" The country was much over-run with long flags, but the water was of no depth, excepting the two arms beforementioned. Most of them were half a mile over.

Having arrived at Verride, I sent the soldier to draw rations, but it was too late. Standidge, the commissary, sent me word to come, and he would furnish a supply of my wants. He was very kind. I was regaled with a bottle of English porter,

March 11th.—I set off for Lavos, passing a very woody country, and one river. We were obliged here to take guides, two of whom, in succession, made their escape, by running into the woods, in turning an angle of the road. The trees stood so thick, that all pursuit was vain; on the third, we kept a very strict look out, and he conducted us to Lavos, eight miles.

Here I met my friend D. A. C. G. Macleod, in charge of the 4th Dragoons, under the command of Lord R. E. H. Somerset; they were stationed here. This village lies among sand banks on the sea shore, opposite to Figuero Roads, and the mouth of the Mondego—the houses are scattered about with no sort of order.

We were very glad to see each other, and Macleod gave me a bed in his own house: he kept a lady, named Margaret, a very termagant for temper. For some time she behaved very well, but broke out one day at dinner, when Macleod happened to say something that displeased her. She then took hold of the tablecloth, and madam sent everything on the floor, soup spilt, a smash of dishes, glasses, &c. This, to her, was genteel, and in style; and that night she got drunk with brandy, saying, it was the finest comfort in nature. Soon after my arrival, Macleod was obliged to set off for Lisbon, leaving Anthony, a Portuguese, Adeney, and myself. We all procured billets in the same house, that of an old *Padras*, who, I fear, was a crafty old rogue.

March 25th.—Adeney, Anthony, and I, set off, and crossed the Mondego, at its mouth, which is not more than two hundred yards wide, but enlarges to near a mile when you are in the harbour. The entrance, which is dangerous, is defended by one four pounder that cannot be of use, as the wall is much too high for it. With large guns the place might be defended for a short time, but they have none mounted; nor are the works strong on any side.

As you enter the port, you see, on the left, a handsome town, with a fine market-place, and two or three churches. It is a large place, and there are several good houses in it. In the vicinity are very extensive salt works. The salt water is let in by small canals, into square places, banked about four inches high with sand, and about six yards square. The water lies on till dried up by the sun, when the salt is left behind. It was here Lord Wellington landed, on the 1st of August, 1808, to commence his arduous campaigns.

On the 17th of April, Macleod joined, and gave me my card of entrance into the commissariat from the day I had joined; this was very satisfactory. The same day, our regiment marched to Verride, on our route to Oporto,—eight miles. Being now settled in my new situation, I shall be able to re-new my observations. On this day's march, as Adeney was cross-ing a river, on horseback, his horse lay down in the middle of the stream, to cool himself. We passed this day a dangerous ford that I had been over before in a boat. The day was warm, and being comfortably established, it made my mind easy.

March 18th.—To Perreira, eleven miles, a very neat town, distant from Verride two leagues and a half. But, before I pro-ceed further in my narrative, I must revert to a large convent in Verride. Though a religious building, yet was it a place of pleasure and recreation, for the monks of the order of Santa Cruz, of Coimbra. The monks are conveyed to and from each place by boats, as the Mondego, which runs through Coimbra, washes the walls of this convent. The whole is laid out in the most luxuriant style; and there is everything for amusement that fancy can devise.

Among the rest, I saw a table resembling a billiard table, but with twenty or thirty pockets instead of six. What the game was I forgot to ask. The table was most exquisitely carved and gilt—the gardens too were a great attraction, and, at one end, there was a fine bowling green. The apartments are laid out rather plain, but the situation of the convent is delightfully chosen. There were very few monks present at this time, as they only came in summer; and it being now winter, a few only were left to take care of the place.

One of, the monks assured me that, on a fine summer's evening, they can hear the vesper bell of their convent in Coimbra, sound, and float down the river, though a distance of forty or fifty miles, in a direct line, without including the turnings of the river. There were two very valuable paintings here, by Rubens. One was the massacre of the monks of Santa Cruz, by the Moors. The expression of the countenances is inimitable. The sweet serene aspect of the monks, contrasted with the ferocious character impressed on those of the Moors, standing over them, and butchering them in a cruel manner, must ever excite the most poignant feelings. The second piece was a priest in the act of writing a letter—he is in a thoughtful mood; the countenance intimates that he is a little perplexed about his subject. The back-ground of both these pictures is well shaded, the parts retire in distance and at leisure; exempt from that abrupt termination which, too often, is chargeable on more modern artists.

March 19th.—*To* Cantanheide, fifteen miles. The road to this place is nearly over a heathy common, except where we crossed the river Mondego; and the late rains obliged us to ford seven streams or communications with this river. On the opposite side we landed, as I may call it, at Tentugal, a respectable town, in which the 2nd Germans now lie. Here Anthony left us for Lisbon, having quitted the commissariat, and Adeney and I became mess-mates.

March 20.—To Agueda and Sourdao; twenty-six miles; two good villages—Agueda is the best. These villages being much crowded, I went to another about half a mile further, on the same hill. These, with some others, lay embosomed in a valley surrounded with hills of a luxuriant appearance; they seemed, in a manner, shut up from the rest of the world. The plain at the bottom, is about two miles long, and of the same breadth; the river Agueda, running in the centre, supplies the villages with water.

On my arrival at the small village, I found it a high festival with the inhabitants; they were all in their gayest apparel, and many had masks. They had, it seems, cut, the day before, an immensely tall tree, quite straight, and lopped off the branches. They then set it on end, in the ground, opposite one of their chapels, having first decorated it with festoons of laurel to the top. Several of the branches were then taken and planted like young trees. A rope was tied to the pole, and running through the arm of a tree opposite, the end of the cord hung down, guided by a young man. The rope being lowered in the centre, a live cock was fastened to it by the legs, and hoisted up again.

The players, with swords, were all alert to jump up and kill the cock. At last, one of superior agility, won the cock by killing it. The cock, in the progress of these manoeuvres, was frequently lowered to allure the attempts, but instantly hoisted up again. In the next place, they buried a cock all but the head, and a person blindfold advancing from a distance with a sword, endeavoured to cut off the head at a blow; but, though many attempted, it was long before one succeeded: as before, he had the cock for the prize.

At each interval between the prizes being won, the bagpipes played, in a wild stream of harmony. Some of the performers behaved with irreverence in the church, which rather surprised me, as the Portuguese, in general, professed religious veneration for holy ground. In the evening there was a general dance on the green, with bagpipe music. The people here seemed truly innocent in their manners, and easily pleased with the character of their rural pastimes. It often made me recollect the pastoral scenes described by Cox, in his tour in Switzerland.

March 21st—To Oliveria das Ameas, twenty-six miles. The road commanded an expansive view of the sea and of Oveiro on the coast, a large and fine town with several churches.

March 22nd.—To Villa de Feira, five miles. This sequestered place is swallowed up among intricate mountains and woods; the country fertile in a high degree. I had nearly lost myself several times; but, at last, Adeney and I found the way out. The inhabitants of this district seem to be more civilized than any in Portugal. The houses were clean and well furnished; and the people, in general, appeared to have been better educated—a schoolmaster here, to instruct his pupils, sent up, at night, several air-balloons.

On a hill over this town, are the remains of a Moorish palace, it has a romantic appearance from the town. This place is about sixteen miles from the sea; we halted here until the 27th, when we marched for Oporto, sixteen miles, a city far surpassing Lisbon and Coimbra, in point of beauty. The first thing which strikes a traveller, is a general cleanliness,—also the evenness of the houses, and uniformity which reigns in each street. It is situated on the Duoro, a few miles from the sea, and has a bridge of boats which open in the middle, for the passage up to St. Joas de Pisqueri, Lamego, &c.

The convents here are superior to any I have yet seen, and, as usual, occupy the greatest part of the town. On the northern side of the river is a part called Villa Nuevo de Oporto, or the New Town, inhabited by coopers and smiths, of whom the number is immense. Oporto is very large, and our English company reside here. They generally purchase the vintage some months before it is pulled; making the wine on the spot, and floating it down to Oporto, where they doctor it for our market.

As to their wine, the juice of the grape alone is not so capital as is imagined, being rather insipid. There is one street here called Rua des Ingleses, which may, perhaps, rival any in Europe; the houses, numbers 1, 2, 3, compose the English hotel, and a noble one it is. Oporto very much resembles the towns in England, and one eighth of the inhabitants are thought to be English—the wine company giving employment to so many; and to this company may be mostly imputed the commercial prosperity of Oporto.

Throughout Portugal, the orders of Santa Cruz and Santa. Francisco appear to be the richest. The chapels, in general, are the greatest ornament about them, and the gardens are laid out in a superb style. One convent here is on an immense perpendicular rock, on the south side of the town, and has a truly grotesque appearance; I was billeted just under it. The town lies on the side of a hill, like Lisbon and Coimbra, slanting to the river. The streets are very good, with many fine houses.

There is a great trade, and shipping can come up to the merchant's doors with ease. The streets are lighted with lamps, in the English mode, and the houses do not look so much like prisons as those of Lisbon. The great iron bars to the windows are not much in use. They are built with stone, very high, many being seven stories. There is an excellent fish-market here, and a good landing place, almost all along the northern bank of the river. The inhabitants are less reserved than those of the south, as their intercourse with the English makes them acquainted with our manners and customs, some of which they adopt. It is rather singular that the port wine is very bad here— nor is it like the wine we have in England; the English company monopolize all the best for exportation. Adeney and I refreshed with a bottle on the morning we started.; but it was not at all to our taste.

March 28th.—To Santa Tissima, a poor place, nineteen miles from Oporto. There is a large convent here, the monks of which gave a dinner to some of our officers. A fine river is seen meandering through this place, with a bridge over it, which throws open some scenery up the river, extending over the romantic gardens of the convent. Passengers pay a trifle on passing the bridge; but the military are exempt. Our troops, presume, had not been often in this neighbourhood, as the people seemed overjoyed to see us, which is not the case where our detachments had often frequented. My landlord would insist on giving me my dinner and breakfast, with plenty of wine; he testified some regret at parting with us. The roads to this place were, in some places, up to the bellies of our horses in mud.

April 29th.—To Caldas and St. Antonio de Taipas, a miserable place, about seventeen miles, hardly worth mentioning as a village.

We were now ordered to proceed to Guimaraens instead of Caldas, and accordingly Adeney and I jogged on quietly, till, finding it very warm, we went under shelter of some trees, where we dismounted. As we had purchased a pack of cards at Oporto, having them in our provision bag, we sat to play at Beggar my Neighbour, and continued three hours at this one game, without loss or gain on either side. When we reached Guimaraens, we waited on the Juis de Fora, but learned, to our mortification, that the regiment had moved forward to Caldas, and we had to push briskly for it, to get in time for our dinners. Guimaraens is a very handsome city, almost as large as Oporto. In one square, we saw as fine a range of houses as most in Europe. It also contains the picturesque remains of an old Moorish palace and castle, about eight hundred years old. We wished much to stop here, but were obliged to be with the regiment, and has no time to make additional remarks.

On our arrival at Caldas, we were again disappointed, as we were billeted at St. Antonio de Taipas, two miles distant, where we arrived at last. Macleod having some company the evening after our arrival, it was near seven o'clock before Adeney and I could get away. The night was extremely dark, but we expected we should know the way; but we soon found our mistake. The houses here were all separated; each had a particular name, and in this straggling way of arranging the village, it was five miles in length. Not a house but what had a distinct farm belonging to it.

We had not gone far before the rain began to fall, and now we were compelled to grope as well as we could with our hands. At last we came tumbling down small precipice together. After shaking our ears, we started again, but stumbled into a ditch of water. After three hours' upsetting, we came to a miserable hut, the people of which would have conducted us home, had we recollected the name of our house or people; but, comfortably billeted, we seldom enquired who were our hosts. Now we paid for our inadvertence, for the people not knowing where we lived, nor we ourselves, circumstances obliged us to put up this night on a bundle or two of Indian corn straw, and rest, as we could, in our wet clothes; but this did not prevent us from enjoying a sound sleep.

Next morning we found our way easily; our servants had been at Macleod's in search for us; but when they heard all the particulars, I could see them trying to suppress a laugh at our blundering. Indeed, the country was full of hills, all nearly of the same shape, and we even had gone wrong in the day-time, the road or path being so intricate. Caldas is celebrated for its mineral waters, both hot and cold, arising out of the earth from the hot baths. You see a vapour ascend from the water, which tastes like rotten eggs. The cold bath will turn stones white, and sparkles on coming out, like cider. A fine beautiful sand also oozes out of the rock, which sparkles like silver, and we used it to dry our writing.

While we remained here, we made an excursion to see Braga, another town, as large or larger than Guimaraens. It has a fine market-place, and contains many capital buildings. The road to this place from Caldas may be considered as truly romantic. There is an immensely high mountain, over which the road goes. On the top is a chapel, by the roadside, from which you can see as far as the eye can reach. Under you, at one side, lies Guimaraens, and appears at the foot of the mountain, though many miles distant. On the other side appears Braga, really at the foot of the mountain, but seems so near, that you would imagine you could almost jump into it, though two miles down the mountain.

The pinnacle you stand on runs off before and behind, in one long line, until lost in more gigantic hills. In distance, in the back ground, lay rugged tops of mountains, some of them soaring far above the clouds. While we remained here, we were appointed to seize all the live cattle we could find; and being frequently out, the commissary of the 5th Dragoon Guards came, by accident, to my billet, and seized five cows, for which we always paid. The host told him there was an officer billeted on him; but it did not signify, and he was ordered to come for payment next day.

When I came home the family came thronging about me in tears, begging me to intercede for their cows, or they should be ruined. I learned from his receipts that it was my old friend Standidge who had taken them, and I presently gave them a note to him, when he returned them all. What joy did this occasion in the poor distressed family! The children kissed me in their transport, one of whom was a fine young girl of seventeen. The poor father cried with joy.

After this everything their house and garden afforded was most cheerfully given to us; confectionary of every kind was purchased for us, which we distributed among the children, and as eggs were in plenty, and fruit, these we accepted, for I was immoderately fond of eggs. To buy them, we might have had fifty for a shilling, so that I was recompensed, but not bribed, for serving them. There is a kind of etiquette observed among the gentlemen of the commissariat, not to interfere with each others' cantonments, and this was a reason why the cows were so easily returned.

We remained here until the 13th of May, when we moved forward to Fafe, fourteen miles, over the most awful mountains I had ever yet seen. We were, at one time, literally above the clouds, at another almost immerged in the valleys. One-third of our horses dropped their shoes, the roads were so bad. We were often going up and down such steep declivities, that we shuddered to look after or before us, for fear of getting dizzy from the horrors of the immense gulfs below, and the overhanging crags above. Fafe is a tolerably good place, selling all the necessaries, without sharing in the luxuries of life.

May 14.—To Guanderalle, twelve miles; a poor place.

15. —To Ribera de Pena, sixteen miles; passed two rivers: the roads dreadfully bad the last two days, lying all the way over mountains, which horribly fatigued us. But we are now beginning to descend a huge chain of mountains.

16.— To Villa Pouca, a good town, 22 miles. A fine prospect here, overlooking an immense extent of country.

17—Halted. 18. Argerise.

19,20, 21.—In camp, each day in the woods, forty miles.

22.—Braganza. A family here, and the town, have given a race of kings to Portugal; seventeen miles. A handsome place, but small, and not much worth seeing.

It has, as usual in all Portuguese towns, some old Moorish ruins, and a market place.

23, 24.—Halted.

25. —Camp.

26.—Ceifas Camp. This day we cleared the boundaries between Spain and Portugal, and left behind us all the bad roads.

As we entered Spain, it was curious to see the difference of the roads. From scaling the most frightful cliffs we now fell into as level a country as any. The roads were finely sanded, and as even as a bowling green; but there was hardly a tree to be seen; the whole country, for a tract of forty or fifty miles, shewing one continued field of barley, rye, wheat, &c. Here and there you may chance to espy the spire of a church raising its head above the plain, and over the waving corn, now nearly ripe. The spire is a sure indication of a village, and about the church a tree or two has been planted, otherwise not one to be seen in any direction.

All over the country we could not trace even a bush or a hedge; but one continued field of corn, of various kinds, met the eye, with nothing else to interrupt the view. What a desolate scene in the winter! The people seemed to resemble the Portuguese in their manners, but were much cleaner. Their houses are many of them as bad as the Portuguese, that is to say, built of mud, and covered with bad earthen tiles. The Spaniards are in a manner rude to strangers or foreigners: they seem very selfish, and have not the way of hiding it like the Portuguese.

When I had to pay them (we were generally seven or eight together) and we paid them in different coins, they would stand to argue with each other about the counting. Not so the Portuguese; they take what you give them as right, and dispute about the different coins afterwards. In our payments we never made mistakes, being too well informed about every coin. We found but few in the two nations that are clever at counting above a dollar. Spain, in general, is much better cultivated than Portugal, the latter being infinitely more mountainous. The wine where we are is horrid, and I believe Spain in general cannot boast of superior wines.

May 27.—To Rio Frio, or the Cold River, an indifferent village, twelve miles. 28. To Tabara Camp. I lost Dash on this march, a fine greyhound, and never could see or hear more of him. Tabara is a wretched place, but we were encamped in an olive wood, abounding with pigeons and snakes. The large green lizard is very numerous here, and has been very common for the last three or four days. They are so void of fear, that they came out of the bushes to view us as we passed. They burrow in the roots of old decayed trees, and will bite fiercely when attacked, but never attack first. The largest are eighteen inches long, of a lively green colour, and their bite reckoned poisonous.

There is a small species called Ligartho, in Portugal, which the superstitious account it a crime to hurt, somewhat like the robin in England. They report, and I am told for truth, that many have been saved, when asleep, from the snakes, by these little creatures scratching at the face of a man, to awaken him. Many quarrels had arisen between our soldiers and the inhabitants, about killing them. In one town there happened to be a crane's nest in the top of the church-steeple (a sacred bird in Spain) some of our soldiers saw her on her nest, and made a bet of wine who would kill her, firing in rotation with ball from their carbines.

At last one of them brought her down, which so enraged the inhabitants, that they swore nothing but the man's life would expiate the deed. They threatened hard, but our men presented their pieces, and this calmed them. We were obliged, however, to be on our guard, to prevent fatal accidents. Such are these Spaniards, who will boldly tell you, they are the most enlightened people under the sun; have produced more learned men than all the rest of the world. "Were it not for us," they say, "you would have been all a set of savages."

My notion is, that you never had but one truly learned and great writer, Cervantes, and he ridiculed you, though a Spaniard himself. I do not mean, however, to deny, that there have been many moderately learned men, though not of transcendent genius, in Spain.

Talara wood is very large: here we first got some fine Spanish bread, which was very excellent, and eats like a cake. We shot many hares here, of a fine flavour, and partridges were numerous on the hills, which were now beginning to be visible again.

May 31.—At half-past twelve in the morning, the bugle sounded to turn out, which was unexpected, but at one we were mounted, and moved forward. As we were informed the French were near, we kept close. About eight in the morning we came to a hill which overlooked a fine plain, gently sloping to the river Ezla. On our mounting the hill, we saw many of our infantry camps, each division separate. The troops were in full view, returning to their different camps, the band of each regiment playing. These troops had been sent, during the night, to take a bridge over the Ezla, but on their approach the French blew it up, so that we must now look for a bridge elsewhere, it was a fine sunny day, and all the troops seemed in high spirits.

Over the river the ground rose again in a gentle slope, and we had a view of part of the French encampment. Our brigade, under Sir William Ponsonby, now moved off, and, about three o'clock, came up with the infantry who were passing the river on a bridge of pontoons, while the baggage passed over on another. Here was a scene of jolly confusion; the cavalry forded the river, and the commissariat bullocks swimming over by their side, I got over on one of the pontoons, very luckily.

The German infantry floated higher, up, but many unfortunately lost their lives in the attempt. About eight o'clock I reached our encampment, having this day marched forty miles, and we were twenty hours on horseback. We took a French piquet of fifty men, who were surprised, not expecting us over in the way we crossed. During the night the whole army joined, also Lord Wellington with his wing, in their way having retaken Salamanca. During the late winter, the French had been fortifying the road from Salamanca to Valladolid, and this induced Lord Wellington to move in a more northerly route, which would bring him in the rear of the French, and, at the same time, avoid the works they had now uselessly constructed. There were some French divisions in front of us, whom we drove along before us.

June 1.—Kept advancing, and the French retreating: the roads were delightful, but all the towns lay nearly in ruins, as the French had destroyed them. We halted in camp, near a ruined village, called Couvilhas, where Adeney being, as usual, tedious in dressing, I cut all the tent cords, and it came down on him, so that he was compelled to finish dressing in a drizzling shower, twelve miles.

June 2.—To Fuentes Seco, still driving the French before us, who retired, levying contributions on all the towns and villages; distance, sixteen miles. On the 3rd, to a village called Benafarces, nearly in ruins.

On the 4th we moved forward, and learned that some more French divisions had joined. After this we advanced, but slower than usual. On the route our brigade halted, near a convent, when the old nuns came out and invited several of us to take refreshment, but none of the young nuns were to be seen, as they had been secured out of the way. The old nuns looked ghastly. The country we passed in this day's march was of a most curious description.

On the tops of the hills the face of it seemed all heath, as far as you could see, and as flat as a table, with no interruption to the sight; but all this was a visual deception, as immense gullies ran between these hills, in which were scattered the roads, cultivated grounds, villages, &c. When down on the proper road, the whole country wore a different aspect; it appeared very hilly and intersected. I can only compare it to a table with several grooves cut in it: in these grooves, each of them three or four miles wide, would be the towns; at the bottom of the cavities the rivers.

We arrived, in the evening, at a small grove called Camp de Epino, attached to a part of the garden of a convent, which lay in ruins. It had been a most beautiful structure, but the French destroyed it, for not being able to pay a contribution levied on it. The French had bombarded the place from the top of the hill on which it stands. The building must have cost immense sums, and particularly the chapel, as the remains testify what it had been. Here were the tomb and monument of Pope Urban the Eighth, with the mausolea of several ancient kings and queens. The convent was away from any village, a circumstance not usual in Spain.

The monuments had been all destroyed, and the very tombstones and bodies taken up by the French in search of plunder; scarcely any thing was left but the inscriptions. In the grand hall were the portraits, as large as life, of all the superiors who had presided over the convent for a length of years. Some of these remained entire, but the best part had been destroyed by the cannon-shot. They were matchless pieces in their kind, but were painted on the walls, and could not be removed. Indeed, little now appeared but the bare shell. The Spaniards had collected several piles of the bones, which they approached with great seeming reverence.

I walked through these monuments of destruction and French rapacity, with pensive reflections on the transient character of worldly grandeur.

5.—Camp, nineteen miles.

6.—Camp, sixteen miles.

7.—To Fuentes de Val de Pent. Here was a Moorish castle, from one of the towers of which a winding staircase led, from top to bottom, the entrance at the top. Where this winding stair-case ultimately led to, no one could or would tell. We went down it, and found it communicated with some large caverns under the castle, and then branched off in various directions, but we did not care to pursue the investigation. We wished, however, much to know where these led to, but their end or object seemed to be also unknown.

On our march this day, we drove the French out of Palencia, a very fine town. The nuns, as we passed the convents, thrust their arms out of the lattice work, and waved white handkerchiefs for a welcome, but we could not see them. We had, however, a fine view of the French army, now in full retreat, filing along the' top of a hill.

8.—Camp, thirteen miles.

9.—Santago Camp. The town in rains, and every individual thing shattered in pieces.

10.—Aranillas, eighteen miles; in ruins. Some of the inhabitants lay dead in the streets, who had been shot by the French in their way through.

11.—Villa Beta, sixteen miles.

12.—Camp, sixteen miles. In the last few days' march the country was every way agreeable, and the soil uncommonly fertile. In one place provisions were so cheap, that I purchased a thousand quarts of wine for thirty dollars. Meat hardly to be had. The country was now getting hilly.

June 13.—We moved forward. In this day's march the baggage mixed pell-mell with the troops, the greatest part of which had scaled the top of one of those flat hills already mentioned. On out advancing to the edge of these hills, we found a body of thirteen thousand French before us, who never expected in this point. Only Major Butt's troop of artillery had come up, with the light brigade of infantry, and most of the cavalry. Another brigade of artillery soon arrived, when the two brigades opened on the French, who were passing the bridge over the Pisuergo.

The French moved as leisurely along the road, to cross the bridge, as if they had been on the parade. Our heavy brigade of cavalry were too near, when the French fired a volley at them, and wounded Captain Chitivell of the 3rd Dragoons, and four men. Of the French about sixty were killed before they could clear the bridge. They got over a brigade of artillery, which formed, and they began to fire away at us, but every shot missed. To me it seemed a wonder that, after the many rounds we fired, so few were hurt.

When they were all over, they marched away, first blowing up the bridge, and some others. What hindered I know not, but I have often thought we might have cut them off, by intercepting their passage at the bridge. Most of the men on the ground were of this opinion. Being with Major Butt's brigade, I found that all our shot went over their heads. But now for the *horrida bella!* the very first shot the French, fired from an eight-pounder, hit the muzzle of the gun on which I was resting, but flew off in an angle, passing near nine or ten men, without doing any mischief. We turned to the left, and advanced to Arranillas de Camilla, but were roused next morning by the blowing up of Burgos Castle by. the French, to hinder us from getting possession of it, as a place of strength. We had here a view of Burgos, and could see clouds of smoke rolling over it.

On the morning of the 14th we found our route changed to a northern course, to cross the Ebro, at Miranda de Ebro;

the French, meanwhile, were blowing up the bridges, by whole-sale, In their line of march. Arrived at Huermecis, twenty-one miles.

15.—To Villa Lien, twenty-four miles.

16.—To Medina, ten miles; a fine large town. We crossed the Ebro this day: the passage lies on the east bank, with precipitate cliffs impending, which almost meet in some places, and form a kind of natural roof. The road winds along the river for about a mile, when it turns off. Some of those natural arches were from three to four thousand feet above our heads. The cavalry were obliged to lead their horses through, as, in some places we were on a level with the river; and in others were three thousand feet above it.

17.—San Lorente, fifteen miles.

18.—Camp, seventeen miles.

19.—Camp, seventeen miles.

20.—Camp, twenty-three miles. During the last four days' march it rained incessantly. The country was one continued field and hill of mud; the dress of our soldiers was hardly distin-guishable; and as for the difference of officers and men, it was dif-ficult to say which was which, The French army, by this time, had united, and, in their march, destroyed every village: nothing was to be seen but one picture of universal havoc and desola-tion. The inhabitants of the country had fled to the mountains, and a horrible time they must have had of it. I found myself unwell this evening, from being so constantly drenched with heavy rains; went to bed in my tent, but could get no rest; my bones ached intolerably.

There was very heavy skirmishing the whole of this day, and when we were joined by Lord Hill's corps, consisting of our 2nd division, with some cavalry and artillery, I expected it would bring on a general engagement; but night coming on, and the rain pouring down in torrents, it made both sides very glad to seek a little rest All things now seemed preparatory to a general battle.

The place where we were in camp was in a wood on the side of a mountain, close to a village, still smoking, and in ruins. The whole of the French and English armies lay on these mountains, and on those opposite, with a large valley in the middle space. The mountains ran in a straight line, one row on each side the valley, and the valley might be about twelve miles in length. The French were in possession of the eastern end of the valley, protecting Vittoria, and we of the western. These hills, were very lofty, particularly those on our right, where our light division was planted, with part of it in the valley; but, in the advance, the principal part of the cavalry were on the side of the hill with us.

The country, to the very tops of the mountains, was covered with wood; and, when the skirmishing ceased, we took up our ground. The men everywhere now began making large fires; every ten or twelve men having one to themselves—the French did the same. The Spaniards, by this time, had come up, and they fell to making fires; so that, with the Portuguese in addition, such brilliant illuminations were seldom seen. But many brave fellows who were highly entertained with the scene, were never to see the sun again set, or contemplate such another spectacle. The mountains, on our right, were in the clouds, and the lights at the top glistened but faintly through them; but, in the valley, and at the foot, and half-way up, the lustre exceeded that of any ballroom ever so gaily illuminated.

Thus were we circumstanced the night previous to the battle of Vittoria. The French were encamped so near us, that the valley, not more than twelve miles long and three wide, was covered with 300,000 fighting men of all grades and nations. The commissariat had orders to issue a double allowance of rum to all, and the men were in want of nothing, as Lord Wellington had ordered three days' provision to be issued that night.

The night of the 20th, I missed Adeney; he had fallen in among the French, and was forced to lie under a hedge, all night, in the rain, within pistol shot of a French sentinel; but as soon as we had driven in the French outposts, next morning, he was liberated, and returned before we marched.

June 21st, 1813.—After a dead silence of some hours, except the neighing of horses, and talking of the men over their fires, which was a hermit's silence compared with what followed, we were all of a sudden on the alert, hearing a cannon shot in our front, and the popping shots of our advanced skirmishers; this was soon answered by the French. After this, one continued roar of musketry announced the commencement of the action; the whole army was soon on the move, and the French disputed every inch of ground. For a length of twenty-six miles, this day, it was a hard fought arena.

We drove the French along the valleys and hills, the last of which were of such a height, that it seemed wonderful to me how we could get cannon up; but we actually did. The day was fine, not a cloud to be seen. We drove the French from every position, but there were only three points they seemed determined to keep: these were, El Pueblo, Gomrah Mayor, and the town of Vittoria. El Puebla, cost us a number of lives; so did Gomrah Mayor;— but, at Vittoria, they made no stand till they had passed it, when they turned their battering cannon on us, who happened to be on the ground. But this artillery fell afterwards into our hands,—thirty-four pieces, with eight howitzers. Two of the cannon were eighteen feet long, and sixty pounders; and the rest little inferior as to calibre.

The whole of the French army were, in a manner, disorganized in the event of this action. They lost 169 pieces of artillery, and about 25,000 men. There was a grand dinner to be given on this day, in Vittoria; and the generals had sent for their families and friends from France to be present. So unexpected was our arrival, that we took many carriages of ladies, several of whom were in the heat of the action. The

French military chest was also taken and plundered, mostly by the country people and servants of the army.

A hussar regiment was disgraced for stopping behind to plunder, the booty was so rich; but Lord Wellington afterwards ordered all to be returned, in order to make an equal distribution. Many made their fortunes here. The wagons which conveyed the money, were upset in a ditch; this was taken advantage of. One muleteer had a thousand doubloons in a bag, which he was obliged to return. An assistant-commissary-general, sent some thousands of dollars to England, but it was discovered, and he was ordered to refund; this, I believe, he declined, and he was dismissed for it.

He had, however, sufficient property to make him indifferent about any army commission. Two carts full of gold were upset on the right of Vittoria. I think that it might have been so contrived as to leave some behind, to take charge of the stores and value captured. The French, also, left all their ammunition wagons on the field, many of them full of the plunder and contributions they had extorted in Spain and Portugal. These were seized by the baggage servants and followers of the army. Many of the carriages and horses were carried away by the country people, and the ammunition, powder, shot, and shells, the last ready primed, were strewed, in millions, over the field and roads. The powder casks were broken and the powder loose, so that, if a spark had lighted, it must have been destruction to thousands.

It was reported that the French had been shut out of Vittoria by the inhabitants, and so obliged to go round, right and left of the town; but, I rather believe, this happened from their not being able to get quick enough through, the place, as the gates were narrow. It was on this movement of the French, right and left of the town, that they lost most of their artillery, which was upset in the ditches, that were deep and full of mud. Here it was, too, that our troops gave them another bitter pill. The enemy had only two eight pounders left, on the night after the battle. The carnage was dreadful during the day, but our cannon seemed to have been more fatal than our musketry. In one wood, on the right of the road, I saw about 509 Portuguese killed, and the French appeared, for a time, to have had the advantage here, as the Portuguese had suffered extremely.

Joseph Buonaparte set out after the action for Pampeluna, which he is reported to have reached the same night. He lost all his baggage, as did his army, and he had only his horse left. The marshal's batoon, of Jourdan, was taken among other plunder. During the day, I was with the baggage, close behind the army. As everyone was eager to learn what was going forward, Lieutenant Burke, of the 48th, came up to me; I had known him with the regiment—he was nephew to Sir Robert Kennedy, chief commissary-general of the army. We had not been long in conversation, when the words " Fly! the French are coming," alarmed all the baggage train.

I was with my own, and wished to save it, if possible, so I kept the muleteers at their places, accordingly; but the baggage of many others was thrown in the road, and lost entirely. Before this happened, the muleteers were lazy enough, grumbling for going so fast; but as soon as it was notified that the French were coming, they turned round, and such galloping and racing I never witnessed. Women mounted on asses were soon knocked into the ditches full of water and dead bodies, on the road side, and a great part of the baggage was upset on them. The servants, through fear, left their baggage in the road, and away they went on their mules, ponies, or whatever they happened to have.

Many of the servants returned to Portugal, never coming back; and many a poor fellow that was looking out anxiously for his baggage, this night, after a hard fight, found it lost to him forever, as the country people plundered it. Such a scene of confusion and dismay, an unconcerned spectator might have thought burlesque. Such whipping, and spurring, and lashing, and thumping the poor horses, mules, and asses, &c.; such a strain of puffing and blowing, cursing the slowness of their horses, and those mounted on mules out of all temper! For, in treating their mules so unmercifully, the creatures would not go forward at step; but moved round and round like a wheel, upsetting all the baggage they came near. Many mule riders left their mules in the middle of the road, in this manner, falling off with the giddiness of their heads, in turning round, and they fled to some mountains, on foot, not far off.

After they had gone on a quarter of a mile, a body of Spanish cavalry came galloping along by us, which made me seriously think that the French were coming; but, what had become of the army? We were soon however, relieved from our anxiety, as some English dragoons came up to stop the baggage, all being a false alarm, said, at the time, to be issued by some persons, to keep the baggage at a distance, as they had found a rich harvest of plunder, and were afraid if the baggage had come on quick, they would have had too many to share it with. But whether it was true or not, I do not pretend to say.

It was now too late for me to get all the supplies up to the regiment; and so I took a couple of mules, with four kegs of rum, and sent them after, as they were two leagues past Vittoria, and I had been very ill all day. I encamped about fifty yards outside Vittoria, near the grand gate. In some of the streets, there were hundreds of dead bodies, and wounded. We gave what relief we could to the people, not rejecting even the poor wounded French, who cried bitterly for water; but we had none to give, as all the water about had been turned to thick mud, during the day. I was much fatigued and slept well. Someone in the night fired off a cannon which had remained loaded; the ball, narrowly missed me, as it skimmed along the head of my bed. So much for the vicissitudes of this day.

June 22nd—This day we went forward to join the regiment, being obliged to go round Vittoria, on the west aide, from the gates being shut, which prevented us from seeing the town.

It was in this tour, however, that I beheld the havoc; the French artillery were upset in the ditches, wheels uppermost, and I could compare the heaps of dead, and the, confusion which must have prevailed, to nothing but the earthquake in Lisbon. Perhaps it was worse, as, in some places, the shells, in bursting, half covered some of the bodies with mud and earth. Here let me consider the many suffering for the few; men slaughtering men, who never saw each other before, and a merciful God looking down on the destroying of lives which he himself had given.

My military friends may smile at this grave-morality; but, on the honour of a British officer, I give my sentiments, that the principle of warfare is not natural to man! It was not till after we passed the town that we fell in with the French heavy artillery. The road now wound through mountains, with a very wintry look, well covered, however, with wood of the pine order. The roads very dirty.

We arrived about half past two at the regiment, encamped in a wood. In this camp Lord Wellington wrote his dispatches, in a poor village called Salvatierra. Next morning commenced the pursuit of the fugitive, along the Royal Road, or Caminha Real, to Pampeluna. The road wound through almost inaccessible mountains, and the weather came on very wet. We arrived, in the afternoon, at a small, wretched village, on the side of the mountains, called, Alchacho, through which our road lay. In some few places I observed large fields of wheat, rye, barley, oats, and Indian corn, which, luckily, in part had escaped both the enemy and us. Abundance was to be had, without the trouble of cutting what was in view, or we should not have tarried to ask any ones leave.

On the 24th, the troops halted, as we were all much fatigued with constant wet and marching. On the 25th, we moved through this range of mountains, twenty-five miles; we were quartered in several little villages, which baked excellent bread for the troops. We passed, this day, about ten or a dozen streams, over some of which were bridges, the waters very rapid; but this I have always found the case, in a mountainous country, occasioned by the quick descent of positions from the hills, which gives an impulse for miles, even after it reaches the plains. I was fixed in the small village of St. Ecaye.

June 26th.—We moved again, the day being warm, or rather with an intense hot sun. The country now began to look well cultivated; but we were often perplexed among the many small rivers we had to cross. The French, by this time, had passed Pampeluna, but left four thousand men there, not having had time to draw their treasure out of it. They, no doubt, thought it might prove a stumbling block to us, as it is a *coup de maitre* in the art of war.

On our approach to it, we found the roads improve; we came to an aperture in a long ridge which got us a fair view of it. The road from the narrow aperture to it is us straight as an arrow, and as level as a bowling green. The country, round-about, is tolerably level, but in the back ground lay the Pyrenees, towering one on another, till absolutely lost to the eye in height and distance. From this spot all the cavalry turned off to the right of the town, while the infantry kept moving on to the left, after the French, who had retired, on the road to their own country, worn down with misfortunes.

I met, this day, an old companion, Lieutenant Lima of the 48th; he had been in a small village with the sick of his regiment. He was apprehensive of the French coming out of the town and Attacking him in the night, as he had no guard with him; the town was not more than a short league distant, and full in view. He was recalled, however, the same day, or be would certainly have been taken. We arrived and encamped in a wood over the town of Tajonar, three miles from Pampeluna. Here I rolled down the hill, in the night, from its steepness, and was awoke. by a sentinel, who was near firing at me, seeing a long white body come rolling down. I went to bed again, and never slept better.

June 27th.—We again set forward, leaving the grand city of Pampeluna to the north-west; grand it did appear to us, but we lost sight of it altogether by the turn of the road. In reference to these roads, I must say, that better I never saw; they were as even as a table, without hills or hollows. The ground had been levelled, by an expert surveyor, previous to making the road; but I shall have occasion hereafter to mention these, when I come to the Pyrenean roads. The day was dreadfully hot, and the baggage of all the cavalry so crowded the road, that the dust, thrown up by it, was ready to choak us. At last, we arrived at the neat town of Tafalla, tempting notice of which we had, by the many fruit-gardens on the road side, as we approached.

Here we had plenty of the finest fruit I ever saw; all kinds of cherries, peaches, plums, &c, so cheap that, for sixpence, a person might load himself. The markets, almost instantly, rose 50 *per cent*, sand I have ever found this to be the case, wherever the English enter. We left this town behind us, and moved on towards Olite, a fine town, but not so large as Tafalla. The country all around, in our immediate vicinity, appeared to be covered with varieties of corn; the land, gently rising in small hills, had an appearance much like that part of Spain we first entered. This day we marched thirty-five miles, and encamped near Olite, in a fine grove of vines; the general staff having taken possession of the town.

June 28.—Marched thirty miles to camp, at the convent of Caperosa;—we this day passed a very fine bridge, over the sides of which many mules, with baggage, had been tilted into the river, and the mules drowned before they could unloose the cords of the trunks, &c. with which they were loaded. This gave rise to much complaint among the muleteers, but it was not attended to, as it was evidently their own fault. For when the bridge was already full of baggage, other muleteers would rush into the centre, and those at the sides were inevitably tilted over the side way (not more than two feet high) into the river. I left them to settle their differences among themselves, with their long knives, which, after all their uproar, they replaced in their pockets.

The convent of Caperosa is on the banks of the river, over which was the bridge. It was nearly deserted when we came, and we quartered two regiments of cavalry in it, with all the staff. It appeared to be an old gloomy Monkish pile. All the interior of the chapel in the ancient Gothic style; the apartments, small and filthy, and the convent nearly surrounded by a wood, in which, however, we had plenty of game, and, curious to say, many wild pigs. These last had become really wild, though of the domestic kind. The original cause we could not find out. Some few were killed, but the gallant and noble General Ponsonby published a prohibition, as they might still be private property.

On the 29th we halted, and had orders to return to Tafalla, as the division of the French army we were in pursuit of had now too far the start of us to hope to overtake them.

And now, after this toilsome march, I shall take a slight view of some things which, in the rapidity of a soldier's movements, have been left without explanation. During our movements, our troops depended on the country for provisions. The villages procured us bread in plenty, and we had brought live bullocks on with us from Portugal; many hundreds, however, died on the way. Rum was brought by mules along with us, but of this we required but little, as the country produced excellent wine, some of which had been in cask perhaps the last hundred years.

Our horses fared the worst, as we could not bring hay and corn with us. These were obliged to live upon the barley, oats, and wheat, all green in the ear, which we found in the fields, but were obliged to cut down for the purpose. Sometimes the inhabitants would furnish plenty of oats and barley, the latter of which they only use for forage, and for these we paid in gold. At several places we had to search every house for corn, and often found it stored in the most curious places. Very frequently the communication was by a trapdoor under the bed, through thick walls, at tanks under the foundation of the house. In a variety of cases, we were sure to trace them oat, but after all, many, doubtless, were undiscovered.

The Spaniards, through the whole of the country we passed, were, in general, dirty. The women usually wore petticoats made of a kind of coarse tick, and they had short bed-gowns, with long sleeves; the men had a dress not unlike ours, but overall, a tremendous great coat, the tail of which they tucked up under the right arm, and threw over the left, letting it fall down behind in folds. This they wore in weather ever so hot; and I often remarked that this coat smelled strongly of tobacco. Some of the Spaniards appeared to be very friendly, others very reserved and morose.

Altogether I found them a most affectionate people, if you can insinuate yourself into their favour, which, however, it was very difficult to do, they kept themselves so retired. These last observations are only applicable to such as had never left their native homes, but as for travellers, voyagers, &c. the very reverse will be found to be the truth. The Spaniards are not only imperious and overbearing to strangers, but are seldom known to unite in the bonds of a strict friendship, even among themselves. The husband continues to smoke, and the wife sits at her work, whether spinning or otherwise. The women have a pan of charcoal under their petticoats, to keep them warm, as in Portugal, if the weather be cold. When very warm, they retire into the shade, as the sun's heat will, in a manner, if too powerful, boil, or at least act upon, the brains, even to the height of madness. This happened, in some instances, to our men, both in Portugal and Spain. The French call this distemper "*un coup de soleil.*"

The houses of the Spaniards are but meanly built: as in Portugal, whole villages are often constructed of mud. To make up for this, almost every village has a church, and often ornamented beautifully. The Spanish architecture in churches is, perhaps, inferior to none; some churches which I have seen in small towns, would match any buildings of their size in Paris or London. How the Spaniards could take so much pains to ornament them, I cannot conceive, for I never had even a faint idea of what laziness was, till I entered the Peninsula.

The Portuguese herein are culpable enough; but are positively laborious, compared to them, and to this, as well as to superstition, may be ascribed the superfluous excess of monks and nuns of different orders. It is supposed that, on an average, one-eighth of the population of Spain and Portugal are devoted to the religious profession. And of all these, three-fourths have hardly anything to do, but live on the best of the country's productions.

How any government, with pretensions to common sense, can mildly look on at such despicable drones, of not the least use to society, surprises me; but religion in this country is the supreme authority, and the king himself must be subservient, and not offend it. Each order, of which there are many, has various and ample resources of revenue; but, in general, they are endowed with large tracts of land; and of this the convents have the most.

There seem to be but few large land-holders in Spain, excepting these. The nobility have some, but altogether disproportionate to the convents and various orders of Santa Cruz, San Francisco, and an hundred others. Of the first two orders there are many ramifications, having in every province three or four, or more, branch convents. The single order of Santa Cruz is computed to contain above three hundred convents, in Spain and Portugal; all of these depend on one another, but their head convents in Madrid and Lisbon receive the greatest share of the revenue, as they draw it from so many minor sources. These convents are under the bishops, and these bishops may be deemed despotic, or at least it is very dangerous to offend them.

Private property seems to be well guarded, and the confines of each boundary marked by cuts in the ground, large stones, or stakes. Very few hedges are to be seen, except near large towns, and these very indifferent. Stone walls seem to be the principal means of defence, near towns, but they seldom rise more than four feet from the ground. Water-courses are often cut, to divide Spaniards carry the produce of their vineyards to market, either in wine or fruit, both of which, with bread, constitute their principal food.

Of meat there is very little used, and even that very poor. The best we found in the country was the Merino (sheep) mutton, which was as delicate as our lamb, but much sweeter tasted. Their bullocks they did not care to part with, as being wanted for draught. Cows were generally killed, when young, for food; but they kept many for milk. Butter was seldom made of it; cheese was frequently, but it was as hard as flint, and had a very imperfect flavour. Their breakfast is chocolate, which is here much superior to any in England. A small cup, containing about half a noggin, a bit of dry toast dipped in it, and then eaten. When it is out, the whole is washed down by a draught of cold water. This was a sort of breakfast I never could relish.

The lower classes have generally soap made of vegetables for breakfast, dinner, and supper; and in some places I have seen the pigs live on the same food with the family, with a little corn added. Their dinners, vegetables and meat, with but little of the latter. Chocolate at night. Wine is drunk all day through, feat it seldom mounts into their head, as they are habituated to it from their childhood. Fruit makes a share of their food, with bread; the latter is excellent, very close-grained, and what we had near the Ezla, more like a delicious cake than bread.

The Spaniards are, in general, very poor; and those that are rich, never do any good with it for their poorer brethren. This observation is not only applicable to Spain, but to almost every country I have visited. The riches of those who are possessed of them, are expended only for their ease and enjoyment; and, provided they can wallow in every gratification, the poor may starve. The rich may often be seen in Spain gambling away thousands. Indeed, the inhabitants, in general, are great gamblers. I have seen the father of a family gamble away his vineyards, wines, houses, goods, even the coat off his back, and leave the room almost naked. When they pursue it hotly, no consideration for themselves or their family can check them; all is forgot in the raging delirium for play.

Tafalla is a large and well-built town; the houses are principally of stone, roofed with red tile. This place not only abounded in fruit, but we had here plenty of ice cream, which, in a warm climate, is, a treat delicious beyond expression. We could get about half a pint for a penny, so that we did not fail to make abundant use of it. We had often met with men, travelling about the country, with churns on their backs, and with handsome cups that looked like silver, but took no minute notice of them, till we came here, when we found they travelled about, selling ice cream. They must have, I think, a pretty brisk trade of it, as they had frequently to replenish their churns, in the different towns; here in particular. But the Spaniards appear to consume a vast quantity of it.

This place once had an old castle attached to it, which is now converted into a market place for woollen goods, the only place of the kind I have had an opportunity of noticing in Spain. It stands on the Camina Real, or Royal Road; and is almost always full of people. While we remained, Sir Stapleton Cotton gave many balls, which the inhabitants of the town returned to us in the best way they could; however, on the night of the 26th July, we had orders to march for Pampeluna, and we set out next morning, at four o'clock, returning by the road we came.

Our orders were quite unexpected, and we lay at our case waiting till Pampeluna would surrender, it being Lord Wellington's intention to blockade and starve it out. But the French army having received strong reinforcements, attacked us and drove us back, till they came in the neighbourhood of Pampeluna, which it was their intention to relieve, and so drew out their troops and treasure. Near my old quarters I left the regiment which had pushed forward, and I took up my quarters in the little village where my old friend Lima, of the 48th regiment, had been alarmed at finding himself so near the French, when left behind with the sick. I had not been long in this village, when a brigade of Spanish artillery came rushing in, at a rapid rate, with horrible accounts; the British army were almost cut to, pieces, and not the least chance of doing any good, the French were in such numbers.

Soon after arrived a Spanish brigade-major, in a dreadful passion, calling and upbraiding the officers and men, as a pack of cowards; but they bore it with much seeming indifference. It appeared that this brigade having fired a few rounds on a French column, were charged by the column; and that our infantry intercepted the charge. This brigade, panic struck with their danger, set fire to their ammunition, which blew up, and they left the field. However, they brought their guns along with them, which preserved some remains of their credit. The Spanish major exerted himself to get them to return, as we could supply them with ammunition; but it was in vain. Here they came, and here they would stop, which they did, till news came of the retreat of the French, when they set out after them.

It appears that our troops had hard work to keep their ground, and were now only collecting and concentrating. Some of our divisions had to march all night through the woods by torch light; when, after a world of difficulty, they effected a junction with the army. It was not till the 29th of July that all the army joined. The gazette will pretty fully detail the particulars of the battle of the Pyrenees. I have to lament my friend L. of the 48th regiment, whom I had seen with the sick in this place. He fell mortally wounded. Also Ensign P. who came up from Lisbon with me; the only two who were killed of the regiment. The last had either one or two brothers killed in the same regiment, in some former campaigns. The family was particularly unfortunate in its connexion with the army.

A slight description of the country round Pampeluna, will help to explain our movements. Everywhere round about this large town, which looks like a mother city among her tributary, children, the small villages are numerous.

Pampeluna stands on a rising ground, with a small descent

from it, on every side. The fortifications are so constructed, as .
to command every hill within range of cannon shot. The hills
about it are not high, but numerous in every direction, the
whole being hills and valleys for about three miles, when the
cliffs of the Pyrenees begin to rise, each tier mounting higher
and higher, till lost in the clouds. On the north side, the Pyrenees are highest, and it was here that the French arrived, on
the 30th of July, when they hoisted a signal for those in the
town to come out and join them. They attempted so to do,
but the Spaniards drove them in again.

All around the town appears to be one spacious field of
corn, except the top of a few hills which are covered with
wood. The Pyrenees here are very bare in this article, which
may be attributed to the vicinity of the town, the people of
which cut it down for fire-wood, and roll it down the mountains. Farther off, the mountains are nearly covered to the
very top: the wild boar takes shelter in the thick forests, with
many other wild animals. The roads to the town are nearly all
straight, and almost as smooth as a bowling green. They seem
to be well sanded and taken care of.

At the east end of the town is an aqueduct, reaching many
miles into the country; I have reason to believe it is useless
now. In one place, it runs through a valley for two miles, and
the centre arches are nearly 150 feet high. It then runs through
a hill, to effect which must have cost immense labour. When
the aqueduct comes within two miles of the town, it runs
under ground the rest of the way. In the town appears a dome
of a church, in the centre, rising above all the other churches,
and pretty much like St. Paul's Cathedral, in Loudon. It certainly has a noble appearance.

The first day we approached the town, we met hundreds
of the inhabitants on the roads, coming out of it, expecting
we should immediately commence the siege. Lord Wellington
allowed all to pass, and the French were glad to get rid of them,
as useless mouths might eat up the provisions, if the siege
lasted: in this instance it proved to be well judged in them.

I felt not a little solicitude for those poor people, thus leaving their homes, and thronging the roads, every one carrying their goods on their back, on the way to any friends they might have in the villages at a distance. Young females of tender and delicate frames were trudging it along, on foot, heavy laden with their misfortunes and goods, and exposed to the rude stare of the soldiers. Many of these had never, I believe, been so exposed before, and I could see through their blushing cheeks, shame and grief in their hearts at the pressure of their necessities.

Our soldiers, and officers too, took great notice of them. The latter endeavoured to enter into conversation with them, but they abruptly turned away and burst into tears, as we must appear like enemies to them, who had literally turned them from their homes. I thought so many jests given on the occasion, quite out of season, and could only turn away with disgust, repeating from Cowper:

'Tis thus, I exclaimed, with a pityless part,
Some act by the delicate mind;
Regardless of wringing and breaking a heart,
Already to sorrow resigned.

These lines seemed truly apposite.

July 28.—I moved all the government stores to a small village, about two leagues nearer Vittoria, named Ororvia. Here I was billeted in the house of a barber-surgeon. I had long wished to know if the two trades were actually combined, and I found it to be the case universally throughout Spain.

During this day's march it rained incessantly, accompanied by dreadful thunder and lightning. Our troops were hotly engaged the whole of the day on the Pyrenees. We could plainly near the musketry and cannon. The smoke arising from various hills that were visible under the clouds, made the appearance as if we were living in fire and water. The lightning was forked, and cut many curious figures in the air; the clouds, too, seemed infinitely higher, at times, when we went down the valleys. In the evening I received news from the troops that determined me to join them, and learned, to my surprise, that it had been a very fine day, and no rain whatever. The clouds were below them most of the day. The heavy firing, I imagine, was the cause of its being wet with us, the explosion having broken the clouds, and the firing, in a manner, igniting the air. Whether this might excite the thunder, I leave it for philosophers to determine.

July 29.—In the morning we set out, and determined, if possible, to join the regiment. Many were not for coming with us, particularly the Spanish and Portuguese muleteers, who were afraid, if the French came down, they should risk the loss of all their property in their mules: at last we convinced them there was no danger, and we set out accordingly.

Having advanced through the valleys, we came to a small village,(almost within cannon shot of the town; and here all the baggage of the army was concentrated. Had the French, in a sortie, made a dash on it, they might have taken the whole, as we had no troops near. Towards evening we reached the foot of a high range of hills, over which we had to pass. When at the top, the sun was near setting behind the Pyrenees, that branched southward. Here we had an ample view of the French and English armies; ours in the valleys next to us, and the French possessed of the highest mountains, over which their camp spread to the very top.

Our troops were in squares, and principally round the villages; in front was a long hill, which we had well defended during the day, having been attacked by the French eleven times, but they were driven back every time. It was now crowned with artillery and infantry; all the small hills were also occupied by our infantry and artillery. Our cavalry lay in the rear, behind all. The French camp stretched up the mountain, as far as the eye could penetrate. Everything was at silent as the grave, and my fancy was ready to suggest that I could hear a pin drop. I now joined the regiment, and found they had not been engaged.

July 30.—This day, the French made their last effort, which was gallantly repelled by our men; they were driven up the mountains, and then down again. The fighting had been very violent the last four days; for the enemy were determined to liberate their companions in Pampeluna, if possible, and in the attempt appear to have lost more men than were in the place. They might be about four thousand, and they lost, on the smallest calculation, that number, at least, in the actions.

Our brigade was ordered to move forward, and as I had no material business to attend, I mounted my horse, and rode to the top of the hill where I had first discovered our array, and from this spot I had a full view of all that was going forward. I was now elevated more than two thousand feet above the walls of Pampeluna, and it was just at this moment that I observed the French on the Pyrenees hoist a signal for their comrades in the town to come out and join them.

The signal was answered by firing a gun from the citadel, and immediately after they issued out in a body, from the gate on the road leading to France. I saw them all out and formed, when our cavalry and the Spanish army advanced down on them, and immediately a very heavy skirmishing commenced. The French fought like lions, just under me, so that I could see every man's manoeuvres. The Spaniards, who were ten times their number, compelled them at last to retreat, which the guns of the town enabled them to do with tolerable order. This lasted nearly three hours on my left, while in the front, on the mountains, the contending armies fought like furies.

When the French saw their comrades issuing out of the town, their fire increased to one continued roar of musketry, the artillery on both sides being of little use in such a rough and rugged region. But when they saw the garrison again driven in, they gave up the cause as desperate, and, by degrees, retired, until the ring was lost in the distance. Our army, taking the advantage of these successes, drove them at length into France. Part of our army now returned to the siege of St. Sebastians, and the operations commenced with double vigour.

About the same time we took possession of the town of Passages, a seaport, where we had communication with Admiral Penrose and the fleet, so that we had plenty of provisions of all kinds from England. The Spaniards and cavalry were left behind, to keep Pampeluna invested, which now began to suffer extremely for. want of provisions. On the 31st, our regiment was ordered into quarters at our old village of Tajonar, where we were but; poorly lodged and accommodated, most of the inhabitants having fled on the first alarm. I determined to pitch my tent, lodge in it, sooner than sleep in the village houses, they were so filthy.

The day we entered it, we advanced a little, to see what we could of the work of destruction, during the late battle, The first spot we made to was a Spanish post, consisting of a small field-work, and a few guns, to prevent the French from breaking out on our side. This, however, they frequently did, and once or twice in the night, took and spiked the guns, out the damage was always repaired next day. We had a fine view of the town, and could reckon eight or nine spires of churches. Having viewed it's amazing strength for some time, we set out for the Pyrenees, two miles distant. Scarcely had we got from under the cover of the redoubt, when some of the enemy began firing at us, at a distance, with their great guns, as if for a wager.

The balls cut round us on every side, and, as we had no business to keep us near, we clapped spurs to our horses, till we were out of range. We then rode up the mountain, on which the French had been encamped the night of the 29th of July, but could see little till we had mounted another tier, when the view of slaughter and death broke in upon us all at once. The carnage was horrible, but most of the dead were covered with straw and green herbs, of various kinds. I saw what terrific effects some of the cannon shot had on the rocks; huge fragments having been broken off and shattered. After riding till our horses were nearly tired, we turned about, and rode down the steep mountains, home.

It was currently reported, in these parts, that the Spanish sentries, bribed by the French) had let a thousand sheep pass into the town in the night. This gained much credit, and I have every reason to believe it true, although the Spanish general either would not, or could not, find it out. After this, we were ever suspicious of the Spaniards; nor did the French spare them, as they made frequent sorties in the night, so as to keep them continually on the alert. It was evident that the French had obtained some provisions, but, except as above stated, there was no other way to account for it.

On, the 6th of August we had news of the defeat of the French, in another quarter, and the surrender of the town of Saragossa to General Mina, the Spanish patriot, who took here five or six hundred prisoners. During the whole of this war Mina distinguished himself as a partisan; he harassed the French in a terrible manner through the passes of the Pyrenees.

The supplies which came out of France were ever obliged to have a very strong guard with them, as, if they fell in with Mina, who knew every pass of the mountains, their capture seemed inevitable. Not even numbers sometimes, could hold out protection, as Mina would take up such positions as to render numbers use less. In this way did he molest them without intermission. The Spaniards in Navarre made songs about him and his volunteers, but whether they respected him for his success, or because their friends principally composed his army, I will not take upon me to affirm.

However, it is partly true, that they did not altogether like the destruction among the French, whom they esteemed much more than the English, on account of their religion. After all, neither the French nor English armies would aspire to be sainted on the score of religion. It is generally thought that more French soldiers fell in this manner of petty warfare, than in all Lord Wellington's general actions added together. After the surrender of Saragossa, Mina turned after the French in the eastern passes, to intercept stragglers from the main body of their army, and here I shall leave them for the present.

Many parties now set out for a boar hunt, wherein they met with some success. It was only in one excursion that I accompanied them. A number of the country people, who were best inured to it, went with us on foot. We allowed three days for the excursion. Each person was armed with a boar-spear, about ten feet long. We were all mounted, but left our horses at the foot of the hills. We entered the forests with proper guides, but none of us seemed to relish the amusement, it was so toilsome. The first and second day shewed nothing but wolves, many of which we shot for our diversion.

These formidable animals would attack us, when wounded, and we could only defend ourselves by transfixing them with our spears. At night we lay down in any house we could find, where we dined or supped on anything we had killed. We had, however, brought plenty with us, which our servants carried on poles. On the second day's journey, we penetrated some woods that I am ready to think had never been explored by man before. Here we could survey a valley, about three miles over, which was inaccessible, and here we had a view of the wild boar in its primeval state. We fired several shots, the echo of which sounded like thunder, returned, went away, and again reverberated in the valley, at our feet, which was inaccessible from its woods and rocks. I was surprised to see the agility of the boar. I had concluded, from its make that it must be very heavy and slow in its movements, but I was now to experience its promptitude and activity.

On the third day we met with a boar, which gave us a fine chace of some miles. I fired at one time, and wounded it, when it sprang towards me. I ran behind a tree, and loaded again, and when it was at the opposite side of the tree, some-one else fired and hit it in the head: it fell, and I finished it with the butt-end of my piece, which I had but little opportunity of firing, as I was obliged to keep moving round the tree, in proportion as my enemy followed, and so to keep him constantly on the opposite side. This boar had two large tusks, of which it would have made terrible use, if we had not disabled it. The animal was about seven feet long, and three and a half high, when standing up. We could only bring a part away: the legs make excellent hams, a little hard and black, but very sweet. This day's sport proved so tiresome, that we agreed to return home, where we arrived in the evening of the fourth day: our horses had arrived before us.

In this journey, we learnt from our guides, that there were many valleys like those we had seen, totally inaccessible to man, from underwood and perpendicular rocks. It appears that, the boar never attacks man, except when impelled by hunger, and this is only in winter, when the trees are stript of their food, acorns, young branches, herbs, and there are no wild animals which he can surprise. But when the snow covers the ground they are left without resource, and then only do they attack man, and but seldom. One half of the Pyrenees is inaccessible, many parts have never been even seen by anyone. This we can readily believe from what we observed ourselves. No maps, whatever, are correct, in giving the points of the mountains, any further than the extreme ones. We had with us the best Spanish maps that could be had, but they were of no use after the first day.

August 8th.—We left Tajonar, for the small village of Viurrum, on the road to the Ebro. There was nothing particularly observable here; and, on the 10th, we moved to Mandagonia, during which, we passed the town of Puente de la Reyna, or the Queen's Bridge, there being a bridge here over a small river. This town appears in a very picturesque situation on approaching it, but has nothing remarkable to show when you get to it. It is surrounded, nearly, by large hills, over which there are excellent roads, in some places cut out of the solid rock. The ascents are made easy by a constant winding round the hills. The town is tolerably clean, advantage being taken of the river which passes through it, and which is well stored with fish. There are also the ruins of a most magnificent convent here; it seems wonderful that it has never been repaired. Also, an excellent market place, well stored with a constant supply of all kinds of provisions. The main street, which is quite in a line, has many fine shop in it, particularly woollen drapers and jewellers.

We found this place the general refuge of the wanderers from Pampeluna; it was full of them. Soon after you leave this town, you have a good view of Mandagonia, situated at the top of a hill, at the end of a long road, of about two miles, laid out in a straight line; but, when you are in the town, you find little to recommend it, but a beautiful church of the Gothic style, mixed with modern decorations. The inside is fitted up in a truly superb manner. We were billeted here on a priest, who was surly, because we did not invite him to dinner, as he seemed to pine for a piece of roast beef we had with us. Our servants gave him a canteen of Irish whiskey, and he mistaking it for *Agoa dente*, or the spirits of Spain, nearly finished the canteen. He was soundly inebriated, and afforded much diversion, though we were glad to get rid of it by his falling asleep. In this state we left him next morning.

On the 11th of August we arrived at Lerin, a town situated on the top of a hill, to which there is only one accessible road for cavalry. The south side of this town ends, by the fall of the ground, almost perpendicular, for two hundred yards. Pedestrians may climb up the steep, anywhere, though not without difficulty. The east and west sides of the town are bound in a similar manner. At a distance, the place looks like a horseshoe, the open end being a gradual descent to the valleys below, through which the road passes.

The country all about is covered with vineyards, the fruit now nearly ripe. On my arrival here, I had the best billet I ever had in Spain, on a family named Tavarez. The son, Juan Baptiste Tavarez, was the most intelligent Spaniard I had ever seen. He exerted himself greatly, and did everything to amuse us. As you come into this town, you are attracted by the ruins of a fine old palace, though not of very ancient date. We went to see it, and our Spanish friend accompanied us.

On our entrance, there appeared to have been only one large court inside, with apartments under colonnades, all round. These were all in ruins, and our companion informed us that, previous to the late war, this palace had been the favourite retreat of the family of Alba, and the dukes of that title; some of whom are buried here in the church. Of the palace nothing remains but the outside walls; the apartments had been two stories high, but the French were so often in it, and again driven out by Mina, and other patriot generals, that the townspeople petitioned Mina to destroy it. As it kept the poor inhabitants in constant alarm, he complied, and now it is a heap of ruins.

Marble pillars of the most exquisite workmanship are seen lying about in every direction, four or five feet deep. Most of the pillars are of white marble. On your entrance through the gate, you descend a flight of steps which brings you into a long passage, lighted by a small grated iron door at the end of it. This, our guide told us, had been often resorted to by the French, escape by, when hard pressed, as the door led to the tide of the precipice which they could well enough descend, in the night, unknown to the besiegers, who had no room to post sentinels on this side. It had, it seems, been used by the duke's family as a cellar.

In ancient times, however, this residence, must have been a place of strength, and this, no doubt, was the sally port. The front of the building exhibited many thousand marks of war, being almost Covered over with musket balls, especially about the windows, of which last, there were only three or four. This front afterwards, with the ground before it, made an excellent racket court, and it became our daily diversion while here. We went, one day, to see the church, the architecture of which is in the light Grecian style; it was elegantly fitted up, and here we saw the monument of one of the dukes of Alba, of white marble, perfectly transparent, though placed there a hundred years ago. The duke is recumbent at full length; his wife beside him, and, at their feet, the statue of a dog, which had saved their lives on some particular occasion.

During our stay, I observed that many of the walls of the houses at the east end of the town, as also the sally port of the castle or palace, had been cut out of the solid rock. These tenements, cold enough in winter, were, at this time, a real luxury, as the weather had set in very hot. I found, on inspection, that the rock on which this town stands, consists of a composition of sand, lime-stone, marl, and of a soft kind of white marble; the latter, when heated, becoming as hard as flint, which durability it will ever after retain. The country was tolerably well cultivated in every direction; indeed, Spain, in general, may be said to be so, though it does not cost them half the labour that it does in England. Were Spain cultivated in the manner of English farming, there is no doubt that it would supply one half of Europe with grain. Of hay, they make but little; and a field of green grass is a rarity the eye is very seldom regaled with.

While in this town we had frequent balls, my house, facing the church, being selected as the largest. All the females came and their friends; also the officers of the regiments about the place, with others at a distance. At these balls there was no supper, only slight refreshments, such as iced lemonade, iced cream, chocolate, coffee, and sweet cake, with plenty of wine. Of these, each took as his fancy led him. The whole expense of one night would not exceed forty dollars; occasionally, we might have 300 present. The dances, very often, consisted of the *fandango*, which the English never attempted; these are too well known to require an account of. The country dances were very elegant when we began to know them, but this could not be done without some practice. The movements are very slow, much like a hymn tune, or, sometimes, the music is very quick, the dance seeming to beat time to it: all too slow for an Englishman. The dances consist in the twining of the arms, the gentleman and lady together; the gentleman turning the lady round, till her back is to him, and then himself, when the arms of both become crossed on their own bosom, the hands of each meeting at the shoulder. Then untwining again, without ever letting go each other's hands. Keep moving, to the time, with a particular step, then down the middle, in the *fandango* style. Waltzing was also a favourite amusement with them and us. These little parties were repeated every Sunday night, being the jubilee day in all Catholic countries; the townspeople and our officers giving them in rotation.

One evening we witnessed a phenomenon while out on the ramparts, as I might term the boundaries of the town, of very livid lightning, which seemed to be over the river Ebro, six or seven miles distant in a direct line. We could not but admire the immense sheets it came down in from the clouds: after a time it assumed a different form, the sparks and electric fluid rushing out of the ground to the clouds. At last, it grew so vivid and frequent, that we ran the risk of being blinded by it. The balls of fire rushing out of the earth and out of the clouds, flew in every direction; some ran along the ground, some darting from one cloud and entering another. In fact, they illumined our whole town, so that we could see to pick up a pin, or read the smallest print. The light was not at intervals, but in one continued glare. Yet we heard no reports of thunder whatever. The inhabitants told us it was common at this season of the year; they ascribed it to the exhalations of the Ebro, as they never had observed it in any other direction: the day had been very hot. It was a full hour before we completely recovered our sight. The lightning rushing from the earth, none of us had ever witnessed before.

A few days after my arrival here, a party of us rode over to Lodoza, a small but beautiful town on the Ebro, over which there was a bridge into Castile. On the road we were surprised, and not a little shocked, at seeing a vast number of human skeletons strewed all along, and about the road. I found, by some of our companions, who were Spaniards, that on this very spot had been a sanguinary action, between the French and

General Mina; the former were eventually defeated and destroyed.

The Spaniards refuse to bury these French skeletons from a principle of revenge for what they suffered during the war, though the French were treated as roughly as could be, when the Spaniards had the upper hand. The Spaniards are all buried. The French are stated to have lost 1500 men killed, which was the whole strength of the detachment, when sent from Lodoza to Lerin to forage. On their approach to the latter place, Mina, who had just arrived, sallied out on them, and, by dint of numbers, surrounded and cut them to pieces. The Spaniards say the killed amounted to 1500, and I should think I saw that number of skeletons.

But, certainly, there were as many graves of the Spaniards; indeed, they confess to have lost 1000 killed; but this seems to fall short of the number of graves. It was, doubtless, a very obstinate action; for, if Mina had 1000 killed, he must have had four times that number wounded. The French skeletons lie in columns, as they fell, having retreated in a hollow square, as the country was very open for cavalry, which Mina had, but the French none; and this was a principal instrument of their destruction. The skeletons also of a great number of horses are lying about these squares, where the Spaniards had charged and pushed them on the bayonet.

The field of battle extends to near a league and a half, from Lodoza to Lerin. How the French in Lodoza could thus neglect their comrades, I am unable to account for, as there were, by the Spanish account, 16,000 men in the town at the time, who never came out to their assistance. The French seem to have revenged themselves on the inhabitants of Lodoza, by murdering many of them.

The town of Lodoza is beautifully situated on the Ebro, over which there is a bridge of thirteen arches, into Castile. There are some very high hills in the neighbourhood, covered with vines to the very top, the whole presenting an unusual appearance.—In this place, we had some of the best liqueurs we had ever tasted. How made and prepared we could not learn, as the host would retain his secret, he being the only one who made them in Spain. Previous to the French entering the country, he was making a fortune by it, but now, like everything else, the sale had fallen off. I never tasted anything like it; I was well acquainted with every liqueur in common use, either in Spain, France, or England. On our return, the night set in so rapidly upon us, that we ran the risk of lying among the French skeletons and Spanish graves, all night, but after a smart ride, we made shift to get to Lerin.

We had frequent horse races near this town; the Spaniards would bet very high on these occasions, and even run their horses against ours, but they never won a race, as our horses were too swift for them. Now I am speaking of horses, let me remark, that the Portuguese and Spanish greyhounds are infinitely superior to the English; this we assigned to the heat of the climate, which enervated the limbs of our English dogs, while the natives were inured to it.

I had two greyhounds, one English, and one Portuguese, and though my English dog was counted an excellent light foot in England, yet he was always left far behind by the Portuguese dog. The English dog died, on our march, before the battle of Vittoria, and I lost my Portuguese a little after, though I found him again on my arrival at Bourdeaux, in France, he having followed the army in the train of General Sir L. C— I afterwards gave him to the general, and I believe he has him still, or may have transferred him to Lord W——, in whose pack I am inclined to think I have seen him. Many of the officers had their dogs abroad with them. Lord Wellington had a complete pack with him, for hunting, for which amusement no country in the world could afford better materials than Spain, though the Spaniards never hunt in the northern parts on horseback.

During the whole time I have been in Spain, I have scarcely ever seen one truly handsome female; they are all either too fat, or complete skeletons, neither of which can exhibit fine proportions. The inhabitants of the kingdom of Navarre have very bad teeth, which, in general, are rotten. Their breath smells frightfully of oil, which to an Englishman is a very nauseating dose, as the oil they use is not that pure Florence which is used in France, but a rank kind, similar to that which is made in Portugal. The reason why the Portuguese oil is not as good as the French, is imputed to the Portuguese beating the olives off the trees with a stick, which bruises them in falling; while the French pull them off with the hand, so as not to injure, and without hurting them. This creates a material difference when the oil is made, of 100 *per cent* in the price:— but the Portuguese cannot be prevailed upon to relinquish their method for a better.

The Spaniards in this part of the country appear absolutely ignorant of many culinary articles of English adoption. Such a thing as a teapot is quite a curiosity. They destroyed one of mine, by pulling out the bottom, to see what was inside, not perceiving that it opened by the lid. I had some spice inside, which rattled when the pot was shaken, and it became an object with them to find out what they were.—I had never used it much, as I not only preferred the chocolate of Spain to any tea, but even used it in greater quantities than the Spaniards themselves.

The town of Lerin is celebrated for its hemp manufactures, in which more than one half of the people are employed. They were now beating it out in the same manner as they do in England, except that the instrument they used was shaped like a two-edged sword. The vintage season set in while I was in this town; the whole country about was covered with vineyards. The vines grow about two or three feet high, never higher; they are not unlike our white currant bushes, of a certain class. In the winter time, all the branches of the vine are cut off, leaving the stump only, about a foot or two high. When spring commences, new snoots spring out, which run to a great length; these soon produce leaves and fruit, which in August and September become ripe. The clusters are then gathered and brought to the house of the owner, who has a large square room, on the ground floor, ready for their reception; this floor has groves cut in the stone, to receive the juice when pressed, which all runs to one point, containing a tube, into the cellar, and there it communicates with barrels prepared for the purpose.

This is the process of making wine. But the way the fruit is first pressed is extremely dirty, as men trample the grapes under their feet, without any covering to screen the fruit. I have seen men with sore feet, go in and trample; and as for others coming in out of the dirty streets, though expressly to assist, their feet all over mud, the vile practice was common everywhere.—After this pressure, the fruit is put into a machine, where it is again pressed into a solid mass, till it becomes of no farther use for wine. After all, spirits are made of the refuse, stronger than any brandy, similar to what we call spirits of wine. The cellars are very warm, when this wine begins to ferment, and no candle must be brought near, or the air would instantly take fire, and blow the house up.

The expense of the inside of the churches in this country is beyond all calculation; about the altar, which is ornamented in the most superb style, with images of various saints; all, in fact, is one sheet of gold, to the very top of the ceiling, and often the whole of the ceiling is gilt. The walls are garnished with pictures, the subjects taken from the bible, or where there are no pictures, the vacancy is often filled up by an image, or a small altar, dedicated to some saint. All here worship different saints, whom they look up to for protection and mediation.

I was invited, one evening, by my landlady, Signiora Tavarez, to spend the evening with her and a few friends, in the Spanish style, and I accepted the offer. On the entrance of the Spaniards, they all throw off their great coats, and take their seats. Then coffee, chocolate, iced cream, lemonade, and sweet cakes, are handed round, of which you take what you please. The ladies then retire, and the men put their cloaks on again. When seated, I was wondering what was to come next, when presently all the men began to take out of their pockets flint, steel, tobacco, &c. They soon made their paper *segars*, struck a light, and fell to smoking, all together, without a single word to interrupt—all puffing together. When dark, it had an odd effect, as no candles were brought in, and nothing appearing but the flame of their *segars* and the nose, which was all over illuminated, from the light of the *segars*. At last, the room became so filled with smoke, that I was fain to take my leave, not caring to be smothered through politeness. At the balls in this country the gentlemen enter first, when they eat and drink what they please, while the priests, who are sure to swarm here, lay in a good store of eatables, and then retire. This becomes a signal to the ladies, that the gentlemen are waiting for them; when they arrive, after eating and drinking, the dances begin.

And now, having made such observations as time would allow, I received unexpected orders to repair to Estella, on another service; and, bidding *adieu* to my kind landlord, I set out, over an uneven country.

Estella is a very fine town, surrounded nearly by mountains. This place was General Ponsonby's[1] head-quarters. There were several convents here, some of which were nearly in ruins. There was also a Moorish temple, which now is a Catholic church, in very good preservation. The Moorish paintings seem very curious, but rough; at least they will amuse at first. The church, with many of the small apartments adjoining, must have been cut out of the solid rock, and cost immense labour. The gate, at the grand entrance, runs up to the very top of the building, but smaller doors have been cut, to use on common days; the great gates being only open on festivals.

In this town are many fine houses. There is an excellent market here, for vegetables, fruit, meat, &c. Fowls are in great

---

1. This is that gallant officer, Sir W. Ponsonby, who was afterwards killed at Waterloo, while giving his watch and a picture to his *aid de camp* for his wife. Being badly mounted, and in deep ground, he well knew it was almost impossible for him to escape, the French cavalry coming down, and no assistance being near at the moment.

plenty, and wine is sold in several houses. A great woollen trade has been carried on formerly with France, but now everything is at a stand. The town appears to be crowded with lazy young monks, lounging about in every ones way. I was very well pleased when I received orders, on the 24th of November, to proceed for Lord Aylmer's brigade of infantry, now stationed near St. Juan de Luz, in France.

Previous to our leaving Estella, we had news of the surrender of Pampeluna. I was inclinable to call on our way, and see this place, but the Spaniards, it seems, would admit no strangers, till the affairs of the inhabitants were settled, and those returned who had left it. We found, also, that on the surrender, many of the inhabitants were found dead in their houses, from famine, as the French had held out till they began to die themselves. There were about 3500 prisoners taken, the remainder having either died during the siege, or fallen in the different nightly forties.

November 24.—We set out, and passed Puente la Reyna, already mentioned. From this place the roads mounted all along higher as we went, till we came on a cliff overlooking the vale, wherein Pampeluna is situated. The mountains on which the battles of the 28th, 29th, 30th, and 31st July had been fought, might be seen in the back-ground. From this spot I had one of those magnificent views never to be met with, perhaps, but in such a region as this. I think I counted not fewer than seventy-nine villages round Pampeluna, some in valleys, and some on hills. Our great height above them made them all appear as if under our feet. The Pyrenees, on the other side of Pampeluna, shone forth in all their wild beauty, perfectly visible, though I dare say twenty miles distant at least.

The district where the battle was fought projected nearer to Pampeluna than any other. Many other ranges appeared behind these, of a blueish tinge, I suppose from their great distance. Others lay behind these, whose summits were doomed to be capped with eternal snows, far above the clouds, now lightly floating through the air. The villages were, in general, white, the houses being white-washed; and when the sun shone, they appeared very prominent. In the centre of all arose Pampeluna, as a kind of supreme mistress of the vale, with the spires of her numerous churches rising above the houses. The great extent of the outworks was very distinctly visible, from their light brown colour, the cannon dotted all round appearing like so many black spots. This town is on the frontiers of Spain, towards France, and an enemy from the latter country could not well penetrate into Spain, without first taking it.

We now wound down the mountain, which was not very difficult, as all the roads here bad been surveyed before entirely formed, and the easiest descents contrived, though in some places, the road had been lengthened in consequence. In about three hours we came to the first valley, after which part of our company, wishing to get forward, left us behind, and this occasioned us a degree of trouble. We intended to have stopped at Irutzen this night, but we lost ourselves in the mountains and woods.

We roved about two hours, and could not even find the road again. At last, we met with a shepherd driving a sheep before him. He told us we were in a very intricate part, and invited us to come and join some of his companions. We did so, but were rather apprehensive that he might lead us among *banditti*. We were soon eased of this fear, as the shepherd showed us his comrades not far off, all round a fire, with their flocks standing and lying about them, like so many children. An excellent fire they had, which comfortably warmed us.

After they had directed us as well as we could understand them, we set out again for Irutzen, which, after all, we almost despaired of finding. We had not gone above a mile, before we again lost our way, and rambled about till nine o'clock, when we were almost minded to lie down in the wood for the night. Hope, however, still led us on, and at length we fell in with a shepherd's cottage, where a letter party of the 10th Hussars were quartered. Here we enquired our way, but were advised to proceed no farther that night, and we thought best to agree to it. They found me a bed, the best that was to be had, and I went to sleep, heartily tired, as we had travelled forty-eight miles this day.

Next morning, we set forward again, and, after crossing a valley, met our party, who had been not a little alarmed, for fear we might have been murdered. We agreed, after this, not to separate any more, during the journey. We were soon again on the Camina Real, here elevated one thousand feet above a river. The rock, on our left side, was perpendicular down to it, without any parapet to protect mules, or anything else, from tumbling down; the road, however, was tolerably wide—ten feet. We dismounted, and led our horses; the rock on the right of us rose three or four hundred feet, in some places, over our heads, to the opposite mountain, which rose perpendicular to the height of the one we were traversing.

After advancing about a league, the road began to descend, till it came on a level with the river, with which it now kept company, sometimes on one side, and sometimes on another. At last we came to a house, curiously seated under the mountain, close by the river side, and here we stopped to breakfast. I must give some account of this, as it is an exact counterpart of many Spanish inns, the situation excepted. Having dismounted, the hostler took our horses to a shed, covered with branches of the pine, which let the air and rain in, or any living creature that had a mind to enter.

There was no manger, and we could scarcely get room for our nags, the place being full of mules and muleteers, who had passed the night there. We then entered the ground floor of the house, which was crowded with mules, muleteers, dogs, cows, pigs, and a number of other things that I had not leisure to enumerate. On our telling the female servant, who was certainly Don Quixote's Maritornes, that we could not breakfast in such a hole, with a scornful look she asked if we would walk up stairs. This we assented to, and began to look about for a staircase, but could find none. Maritornes, seeing what we wanted, presently got a ladder, up which we mounted to the first floor, through a trap-door.

When there, we found a whole posse of muleteers, fast asleep, all round the room, their beds being the trappings of their mules. We took the middle of the room to ourselves, and had some chairs and a table handed up from below. At first we found the trap-door too small for their admittance, when Maritornes, springing up, out of patience, and raising two or three of the flooring boards, none of which were nailed, hauled them through in a trice.

We next inquired for the man servant, to see what could be had for breakfast, when our hostler popped his head up the trap door, and gave us the contents of his bill of fare—bread, eggs, oil, and tobacco, with *agoa dente*. The last we ordered, and directed him to send his master with it immediately, as we wished to warm ourselves. When lo! up comes our hostler again! In vain we asked to see the master; this man, with a humble bow, told us he was the master.

We then ordered bread and eggs, and made some tea with our own apparatus, though we had some trouble to do it, as the muleteers crowded round our servants, to see the process, and it seemed to excite much laughter. While breakfast was getting ready, we agreed to walk out and view the place; and as a preparatory, we filled a glass of spirits each, and had nearly swallowed the dose, when we threw away the glasses in agony, it being spirits of wine, which took the skin off our mouths and throats. From our being so cold, we had no conception of it, at first, till it had gone half way down.

Having made a little promenade, we were highly amused at the situation of the place. The house lay about twenty yards from the river, under the shade of the rock, which had still attended us all along this morning's ride. It was here about a thousand feet high, and many large blocks projected in various parts. We saw the goats fearlessly browsing along the edges of this precipice. On the opposite side the bank rose more sloping, and was thinly scattered with fir and elm trees. I had an opportunity here of noticing some of the inhabitants in the act of transporting their fire-wood. When in want of a tree, they ascend that part of the mountain that lies immediately over their house; here the tree is cut, and at once rolled down the mountain to their habitation. After breakfast we again set forward.

I had particularly remarked the roads in this day's journey, and was almost petrified with astonishment at surveying the labour they must have cost. For a length of twenty miles, they were cut out of the solid rock, in some places forty feet deep. I could have reckoned millions of bores, where the rocks had been blown away from the side, to make way for the road; and when the road was from ten to twenty feet wide, how many millions of tubes most have been bored to bring the road to its present perfection? In some rocks I counted thirty bores, before a level could be obtained.

When the mine was sprung, the piece next the river must have darted away, leaving the solid rock against the bank without injury. The roads, all along, were almost as fine as a bowling green; and they are as passable in winter as in summer. Those leading from Vittoria to France, were all cut up by the French forming redoubts across them, to intercept our passage, but they proved of no use. We passed Tolosa, a large town, this day, and arrived at Ernani, about eight at night, having advanced sixty-four miles this day.

On our approach to this place, the mountains seemed to withdraw, leaving us a very handsome valley open, which was well cultivated. The method of digging here was rather curious. Five or six men or women had forks with four or five prongs to them; these they rose at the same time, striking them into the earth in a line, then they turned up the sod altogether, taking a large piece up, their forks being a foot asunder, or more, when struck into the ground, I heard them singing a tune and keeping time, at this work. At night, I fell asleep, heartily tired, and rose up much refreshed in the morning; yesterday's journey was the last long one I had in Spain.

On the 26th, we set out and arrived at Passages, a seaport, near St. Sebastian, but we had a world of difficulty in getting into it. In some places, rivers to wade through, and in others, up to the middle in mud. Such a road as this I had no previous idea of. One of our mules, unluckily, tumbled down a precipice, and was killed: the baggage it was loaded with was lost in a river. The mule must have been dead long before it reached the river, as the precipice, which was four or five hundred feet deep, was knobbed with huge fragments of rock, against which the poor mule hit, and it must have broken his bones.

On the 27th, we left this horrible mud-hole, as I may call the town, and proceeded to regain the main road, which, after much difficulty, we effected. We now took the road to France, leaving Lezaca to our left, with a most awful tier of the Pyrenees, which terminated the range. A view of this is given. At one point, was a cleft in a mountain, from top to bottom; I cannot pretend to describe its odd appearance. At the top of the highest, mountain, which was over Lezaca, was a cap of clouds by which the country people could prognosticate the approach; of bad weather; some account of this I shall give, hereafter.

We now found the road cut up every two or three hundred yards, by the French redoubts. In some places, they, had created regular field bastions; the. road also was strewed with, deed' bullocks. At last, we arrived at the bridge of the Bidassoa which the French had blown up, with every other bridge in their way. This, bridge was the grand entrance into France, and: about four or five miles from the mouth of the rivers, at which point was the town of Fontarabia, on the Spanish side, and St. Andaye on the French. The Bidassoa became the boundary of the two kingdoms, and now it was that I prepared to bid a final *adieu* to the kingdoms of Spain, by passing over an English bridge. One of our pontoons was thrown across, and over the stone one which the French had blown up. The opposite bank rose very high, with a rising road that wound round a hill. At length, having taken a glass of wine, as a sort of farewell to Spain, we began crossing the pontoons, which we did with rapidity, and arrived, for the first time, in France. Here was the grand and last stand of the French, previous to their quitting Spain, a view of which is annexed.

Having mounted into somewhat higher ground, we continued to advance for about two miles without being able to see very distinctly the extent of our movements, when, at last, we emerged, and soon found the difference of the two countries, France now lay like a panorama before us, to our right, with the ocean on our left, and a view stretching along the Spanish coast to Bilboa, taking in Passages and St. Sebastian, We could distinguish the English shipping, crowding in and out of every port, some at sea, and others going out of sight.

In front, appeared a number of neat French towns, as far as the eye could reach; the villages all beautifully white, the country very well cultivated, and exhibiting a very cheerful aspect, quite different from that of Spain. Plantations of trees regularly interspersed among the lands; many *chateaux* and country houses, as in England, with elegant gardens about them. In Spain and Portugal, I don't remember to have seen one solitary instance of a nobleman or gentleman's residence separate from a town or village, and only one instance occurred of a convent, as already mentioned, the country being, in fact, at the best of times, overrun with brigands. But now, what a different scene! There was, seemingly, here, no ground for distrust, or any fears of the kind.

The soil seemed to be well taken care of, no forests in their original state, but all had a face of regularity and embellished nature. The Pyrenees lay behind us, wild enough, but most of the mountains at this side had gradual descents, while, on the Spanish side, they were altogether abrupt. We passed several batteries on the road, and the fields, all along, were full of straw, indicating where the troops had been encamped. At last we arrived at St. Jean de Luz, a little seaport town, where we took up our quarters, and which, indeed, became the head quarters of Lord Wellington, and all the staff.

We found this day the change of climate, the weather now being temperate, that is, moderately warm, compared to the cold air in the mountains. The roads to this place were excellent, and, after a day of not a little gratification, I went very gay to bed; but, unluckily, had not much rest, from the effects of excessive fatigue, having rode nearly two hundred miles in four days.

St. Jean de Luz is but a poor town, but much cleaner than any of the Spanish ones. This is saying but little of it. The people were much cleaner, but not so the streets., which were full of mud. The houses are built in the antique style, not unlike those of the Spaniards. There is a port for shipping here, which is very ill secured, or rather it lay open to the Bay of Biscay. A strong wall between the harbour and the town, may keep out the waves in bad weather; though I have, at times, seen the waves rush over it. The harbour is so bad that, in winter time, it is often dangerous.

We had, in one night, during a hurricane, thirteen British vessels entirely wrecked here. Some of them were driven up on the sand, above high water-mark; but the waves came forward in a perpendicular body of water, of twenty feet, and sometimes more. The wall, however, served as a defence against an enemy. About a mile on the south side, there is a point running out into the sea, on which there is a tower, named Socoa, but it is of little use to mariners, being intended for a place of strength to defend the harbour. The cannon are at the top, under a roof, the guns running out through portholes. Along the coast, there were light-posts, I cannot call them lighthouses, as they were only lanthorns hung on posts, and these had not been lighted till some time after we had been in possession of the country, as our shipping began to suffer severely for want of them.

This town, properly speaking, is divided into two parts; the River Nive running under a bridge, serves to separate the north from the south part, the latter called Ciboure. The town may contain about 1000 houses, and 8000 inhabitants. It was so full of troops, that I was billeted in a house with three others. The staff of Lord Wellington occupied no small part, and the stores of my brigade lay a mile out of the town, and when I went mere, it proved a task to get at them, the lanes were so full of mud, generally knee deep. The fields too had been completely ploughed up with the late skirmishing.

A rumour was afloat that our brigade were under orders to go and besiege fort St. Antonio, between Bilboa and St. Ander; but the order was, it seems, countermanded. St. Antonio is a very strong fortress, and had about 4000 French; it was almost impregnable, and a seaport town. The French would often hoist British colours, and our shipping not knowing but that it was in our possession, sailed in, and the French would then turn their guns on them, and oblige them to surrender.

Hence it was that they had plenty of every kind of stores, and even some of our clothing; and, at one time, they secured all the hay and corn intended for our army, but this was recovered, on their surrender, a few months after, when they marched out with the honours of war. There was also here a brigade of guards, which, during the battles of 9th and 10th of December, had marched out to action in the morning, and returned in the evening. These actions were merely trials of strength, but we always had the advantage, driving the French into Bayonne again. For the siege of this place we were now beginning to make serious preparations.

When we came here, at first, provisions were very cheap. We might have had a good goose for a dollar; but on Christmas Day they rose to four dollars each, and everything else in proportion. There was but one tolerable inn here, with the sign of Joseph the Second. The waiters, who were women, were very impertinent; their charges, too, were exorbitant, sometimes, from mere caprice, only charging a dollar for dinner, and, at others, ten, for the very same articles. These matters were represented to the commander-in-chief, but the grievance was not redressed; and, from that time, we became lawful prey for the French, who imposed on us in every way. When an Englishman entered a shop to buy anything, if in coloured clothes, the question was, "Are you English?" and the demand would be ten dollars; if a Frenchman was by, and called for the same thing, probably one was the price, and all this even before the Englishman's face. But for the sake of human credit, I am very willing to admit that some French dealers evinced more conscience than others.

One evening, having entered into conversation with the old lady who owned the house I was billeted in, I asked her what she thought of Napoleon. She burst into tears, and told me she had seven sons, whom he had drawn out in the conscript list, one after another, and she believed they were all killed. She had heard of the death of five of them, and, for the other two, she had a presentiment that they were gone the same way. I was much concerned to hear this, and dropped the conversation. We remained here till the ninth of February, when we turned out of the town, to some country houses near Guitaria, which were more convenient, and from which we had an ample view of the sea.

It was from the spot that we had a comprehensive view of the Pyrenees, and of that immensely high point that projects over Lezaca, in Spain. We observed the natural attraction which mountains have, when a number of clouds are floating in the air in various points. This mountain attracted them all to it, whatever point the wind might be in, and as they continued to accumulate to a large cap on the summit, it was a sure indication of approaching wet weather to the neighbourhood. Indeed, I have observed, though not, perhaps, the first, that wherever there is a congeries of many mountains, or of large forests, there is more rain thereabouts than anywhere else. When the cap grows large, the vapour begins to descend, and roll down sides of the mountain, in ample volumes, and the night will commonly bring on heavy rains that may continue three or four days.

From my present habitation I had a fair view of the ocean, and one evening, a little before sunset, I was looking at a fleet of ships coming out of Passages harbour. To my infinite surprise each ship appeared about the size of a mountain, though forty miles distant. The ships were between me and the sun, which was then just dipping into the western ocean. It might have been occasioned by the refraction of the rays of light: however, it presented a very singular appearance.

On the 11th of March, we moved to a small village, three miles from Bayonne, on the sea-coast, in a very pleasant situation. We were obliged to make this movement, as our horses had eat up everything green, and were now living on chopped furze. No forage could be had from Spain, our troops having consumed everything near the frontier. Sorry I am to add, that, according to report, many families perished this winter for want, our troops having fed their horses on the wheat when in the ear, as nothing else could be had at the time. Our army had now moved off, after the French, who were retreating to Orthez and Toulouse. My brigade was left, as forming part of the army in the blockade of Bayonne, together with the Spanish army. Lord Wellington would not let these last come on further, as they bad, in some instances, exercised a cruel authority over the French, by murdering them in cool blood, from motives of revenge. In my village they murdered nine in one night

Being now comfortably lodged, I shall take some notice of this little place. Its name is Biaritz, situated on the seacoast. on a cliff, not unlike that at Dover. This cliff runs about two miles along the coast; it is a place much resorted to for sea-bathing, many of the nobility coming here from all parts of France for the purpose. There is a small passage, or avenue, which shelves down towards the sea; between this and the river Adour, it is all sand banks, on one part of which, next Bayonne, there is a straggling village, named Haut Anglet. There is a church here, which serves for the devotional exercises both of Anglet and this place. Our brigade lay in a camp, down on the sands, in front of Bayonne, protecting the road to St. Jean de Luz. Bayonne is distant about three miles from the sea. Half way between we have constructed a bridge of boats, over which all the heavy stores pass.

Provisions are becoming plentiful here, the merchants arriving from England every day with cargoes. Adjoining the pontoon bridge, is our grand magazine of provisions; there is also another, at the small village of Bocaut, on the opposite side of the river. There are about twelve thousand men in Bayonne, who have been tolerably quiet hitherto.

During; my abode here, the master of my house returned. He was very well pleased to find his house as he left it, and thanked me for it, as he expected it to have been plundered. He was a very intelligent man, and was a retired lieutenant-colonel of the 34th French regiment; Buonaparte had given him a civil situation in Bayonne, to make his latter days comfortable. After I had been some time in the house, and when our acquaintance had ripened into familiarity, he told me the history of his life, as follows:

He had been thirty years in the French army, and not only in Egypt, under Napoleon, but he had served in all his great actions, down to the battle of Austerlitz; but finding himself glowing too old for active field service, he applied to the general of his division, who recommended him to Buonaparte for superannuation. On a general field day he was called out, and Buonaparte questioned him on the nature and extent of his services. He asked him, moreover, his native place, and when he replied Bayonne, Buonaparte gave him his present situation. He had held this three years, but on the English advancing to Bayonne, he moved forwards to Bourdeaux, where, hearing how well we treated the French territory, he had now returned.

When Bayonne opened its gates, it appears that he again resumed the functions of his office. In a conversation relating to the loss sustained by the French, in the course of the wars in Spain, he said, if it were correctly stated, none would, believe it, as the guerrilla bands had created a prodigious loss, in addition to that of the more regular warfare. He told me that in the official situation he held in Bayonne, he was furnished with lists of every man that was sent to reinforce the army in Spain. When his regiment had passed through, in 1808, there were six battalions of a thousand men each, effective, and in the space of five years he had given passports and routes to fifty-four thousand conscripts for his own regiments alone. But when they came and passed Bayonne but a few days before, the whole six battalions could muster only seven hundred and fifty muskets.

A fine subjects this for such a homicide as Buonaparte to meditate on!

During the time we remained here, we had news of the Moscow army, and that Buonaparte had resigned the crown. The same day that we received this intelligence, we forwarded it into Bayonne, under a flag of truce, and I went over to dine with a friend at Bocaut, on the opposite side of the Adour. I remained there till two o'clock, but on my return was not a little surprised and annoyed with a shower of shells and shot from the town. I was now on the sands, and compelled to go on. However I was fortunate enough to escape all danger. Next morning I heard the detail of the affair. The French had laid a plan to surprise us, to destroy the bridge, and set fire to our stores, but they were gallantly driven in again. Here General Hay was killed, and General Hope wounded and taken prisoner. A number of men fell. It was a disgraceful action on the part of the French, as they well knew peace was at hand. The gazette seems to detail this affair pretty fully.

On my rides across the sands, I observed the way in which the French recovered land from the sea. It was by planting stakes firmly in the ground, when the wind sweeping the sand against it, would cover them. Then another row was fixed above them, in the same way, these beds of sand daily accumulating, until it fairly banked the sea out. It seems highly probable that at some former period, Bayonne must have stood close to the sea, and actually appears so in some old maps, but now it lies three miles from it. These sands, after a few years, will cherish the fir, which, in some places, may be seen in a thriving condition. The same plan is adopted all along the coast, as far as the river Garonne. This sort of contexture might also be made use of even to defend the coast, as it rises perpendicular on the sea-side, and goes slanting off towards the land. In case of an enemy landing, a body of infantry might be employed here with great advantage.

On the second of June, the gates of Bayonne were thrown open, and we now had orders to march to Bourdeaux. Our brigade had leave to march through Bayonne, and it was the first that did so.

Bayonne is a very strong town, and, according to report, one of the master-pieces of Vauban. It was here, no doubt, the bayonet was first invented, and from this place it has taken its name. The citadel here is very strong, and well defended. In three different points twelve or thirteen churches are seen, all of them very neat, but not so resplendent or glittering as some of the churches in Spain. The town contains two theatres, about three thousand houses, and thirty thousand inhabitants. The streets are laid out very regular and neat, and the people appear to be very cleanly. There are many delightful alleys or walks for the promenade, on the banks of the river, with large trees to shelter from the sun. The town is as full of coffee-houses as Lisbon, for its size. There is also a fine bridge over the Adour, which connects the two parts of the town together. We passed this, and entered Gascony, moving through the gate of, or rather to, Paris, called by the French *Le Saint Esprit*.

Previous to our entrance into this country, the French had driven away all the cattle into the interior, and removed all the provisions, but the farmers hearing we paid for ever thing, came back, and supplied us plentifully with beef. This was doubtless a treat to us, as the French cattle were almost bursting with fat, and very delicious, indeed, not inferior to the best in England; and we found it the more grateful, after the bad meat we had put up with in the winter. The bullocks which we had killed for rations, were all mere skeletons, without an ounce of real fat on a whole carcass. These had come from Spain and Portugal, and were fat enough when first bought, but after a march of some hundreds of miles, their goodness wore away, and the few that arrived were like shadows. Out of one herd sent us from Santillana, consisting of four hundred head, ninety-two reached us, the remainder having died on the road, from fatigue. Great must have been the expense of supplying us with this article. However, as soon as the ports were opened, the fleet poured in salt provisions in abundance, which we highly relished. But this indulgence could not be taken every day, as the men were but in an indifferent state of health, from the hardships they had suffered, with a succession of wet weather.

This day we marched four miles past Bayonne, and encamped on the road side. The country was woody all about.

On the 3rd of June, we moved on to Castets, through alternate woods and plains.

On the 4th we reached La Harie.

On the 5th, La Boukere.

6th.—La Marets.

7th.—Le Barp.

8th.—Bellevue; and on the 9th, Bourdeaux, which is reckoned a hundred and fifty miles from Bayonne. I have given these together, as the country is pretty much the same, almost to the gates of Bourdeaux. Nothing particular occurred on the journey.

This whole country was formerly called Gascony, but now the part we travelled had assumed the name of the province of the Landes. It was a perfect flat the whole way, the roads very sandy and deep. We lost some fine scenery by coming this way, which was only a bye-road, the grand one running by Dax and Monte de Marsan.

The woods here are all pine, but in many places there are

large plains without any. Plain and wood appeared to succeed, alternately, the whole way. When you first come out of a wood, and look across the plain, you see, at an immense distance, a kind of cloud on the edge of the horizon. On your approach, it becomes more distinct, and, at last, you can distinguish the tops of trees. On a nearer approach, you can see their straight trunks, and so on till you get into the wood. This is a very carious sight; as, when you look into the middle of some of the large plains, the above effect will appear around you in every stage, till lost in distance, growing fainter and fainter till it dies away. From some few parts of this road we had a glimpse of the sea; the shore seemed full of pools left by the tide, and of those there were many thousands, reaching some miles in length. This shore certainly looked the most desolate I had ever seen; it was, for nearly ten miles, all sand and pool.

The language through the whole of this province is Gascon, which is spoken here, I understand, in its original purity. I am told by the natives, a few only of whom speak the genuine French, that in the province of Biscay the same language prevails, and it is unquestionable, that from Bourdeaux to Bilboa, the inhabitants have a language of their own. It is, however, most grating to the ear, and repulsive to the sense. Many who have learned it, say it is very comprehensive.

The inhabitants of this province are very intelligent and clean. Their houses are particularly neat; in one place we met with an inn that would look well beside a palace. The villages, all our way through, lie close together, nor are they very straggling. .The inhabitants derive much of their subsistence from the manufacture of turpentine; they also breed large flocks of sheep, which they sell in the market towns. Their dress not a little resembles that of the Spaniards; but with a short jacket in place of their great coat.

The manner of saving the turpentine is rather curious. They cut a grove of the bark off, for about twenty or thirty feet up the trunk of the pine; this is about two inches wide, and in the summer, the turpentine flies to this grove, and floats to the

SHEPHERDS OF THE LANDS

bottom, where it has the appearance of rosin. This is collected, and it proves a considerable source of revenue. Every year a new grove is cut in the tree, the last year's being of no further service. In this manner the tree is cut every year, till the whole bark has been stripped off, in a circle of rotation. The tree is then left to itself, till it again recovers the bark. This is again cut into; but the product is never so good as at first. Such a process as this must naturally ruin the timber in the course of time, and, in fact, it becomes only fit for firewood. After all, it is the branches only that furnish this article, as from the rosin being extracted so often, the trunks will hardly burn when put on the fire.

The shepherds and country people, in this province, all walk on stilts, some of them fifteen or sixteen feet high. When I first observed them, at a distance, on one of the plains, I was completely dumb-founded to think what they could be. I could only see the man, the distance having done away the stilts. These conveniences are adopted, or rather, they are, in a manner, necessaries here. Many of the inhabitants are shepherds, occupied in attending their flocks, and, as the plains, in many places, are full of a high kind of fern, rising to three or four feet in height, should the sheep get in among those places, would be lost to their owner, as they could not find the way back. But the man, by means of the stilts, being so elevated above this underwood that he can see where every sheep goes, he fails not to act accordingly, by keeping them together.

The stilts answer also another purpose, that of moving much quicker across these immense plains, as, in some places, the church is not less than five or six miles distant. To go there, and return, would consume the best part of their Sunday, which is always a sort of jubilee with them, but with the stilts, the man can go eight or ten miles an hour, without trouble or fatigue. These stilts are made of long poles, with a small projection of a fiat piece of wood for the foot to rest on. The pole only comes up to the knee, being strapped on there, and at the ankle, which makes it firm. They always carry a walking stick with them, which helps them to recover themselves, if they should stumble, which happens very seldom. It amused me much to see with what ingenuity they can let themselves down to the ground, by means of this pole, and not only so, but even lay hold of the smallest thing without taking off the stilts. A shepherd kept up with me, one day, although I was in a hard trot, nor did he seem to subject himself to any inconvenience, more than a person moderately walking on foot might be thought to do.

On our approach to Bourdeaux, the country improved; the whole was now replenished with gentlemen's seats, gardens, and pleasure grounds. A grand relief this to us, just coming out of Spain, where that delectable object, a park, or pleasure ground, was hardly ever to be seen. The weather was pleasantly warm, and I lodged with a worthy family, in Rue Nueve; the kindness of these people I shall long remember. They behaved as if I had been their son, and entreated me to give up my commission in the army, and live with them. This I declined, but had some reason to regret my resolution. They were, undoubtedly, the first wine merchants in the place. At our parting, on my leaving them for England, the family hung about me dissolved in tears.

Bourdeaux is a large and fine city, stretching along the banks of the Garonne. The river is about half a mile wide, and about sixty miles to its embouchure, or mouth, at Verdun. There are many churches; that of St. Michael was built by the English in the days of Edward the Black Prince; and there are still several others that were built by our ancestors. Indeed, I believe most of the old town, as it is called, in this city, was originally built by our kings and princes, when all the provinces roundabout were an appendage of the English crown.

The streets here seem much in the English style: there is one called the Chartrons, of almost matchless elegance and beauty. There are also two very good theatres, the *Comedie Francaise,* and the theatre *Gaité.* The society, too, is delightful.

Along the quays are an immense number of coffee-houses, with billiard tables. In one house, I reckoned eight tables, and I should think that on this tier of coffee-houses, there could not be fewer than one hundred. In some of the princely buildings here the staff of our army was quartered.

On the opposite side of the river the country gradually rose, and gentlemen's seats were profusely scattered all about it. From the town we could see completely into the country, and from the country, a fine view expands over the whole town, river, and shipping. I thought it the most agreeable situation that I had ever seen in my different peregrinations. The ships come up to the doors of the merchants, and the river is navigable, even up to Toulouse, for large boats. In Bourdeaux are large markets well furnished with every luxury and necessary of life, and the prices moderate.

On the 9th, we had orders to embark for England; and having previously provided everything requisite for the purpose, we went on board a Dutch *galiot*, and, on the 13th, set sail for the mouth of the river. We had not been informed that the ships were to tide it down, so that before we got into Verdun Roads, our sea stock fell short. We dined every day on shore, and, at one time, slept there, as the ship had run aground, which it often did. Indeed the whole fleet stuck once in the mud, together; however, the next tide brought us off.

The scenery all along the river is studded, as it were, with gentlemen's seats and well cultivated. About twenty miles from Bourdeaux, we saw the fort of Blaye, with an island finely situated in the river. At last, after eleven days' tiding, we arrived in Verdun Roads, about two o'clock, the river here being about eight miles wide. We got on board of the pilot boat, expecting to sleep on shore, but were unable to land anywhere, the breakers appearing so furious, and the waves rolling in very high from the Atlantic. The town of Royan is very alluring to the eye, especially of a sailor coming from a sea-scene off a long voyage. Next day we landed; but the town afforded nothing remarkable. Here we had abundance of fruit and eggs, all extremely cheap, so we could again lay in a pretty good sea-stock. At length, we set sail again, and passing between the points at the mouth of the river, we left Cordouan tower to our left, and made away for the ocean.

I was informed, in Bourdeaux, that this tower had been built by a young lady, on the following occasion. She was to be married to a merchant, who, previous to the ceremony, had to make one voyage to the West Indies. He had made his will, should anything sinister happen to him, and she was appointed his heir. In his return from the voyage, the ship he was in struck on this point where the tower now stands and foundered, when every soul on board perished. When Miss Cordouan heard of this dismal accident, she caused this tower to be built with his fortune, and adding part of her own. She then retired into a convent, where she immured herself for life, and afterwards died. The tower may now serve to warn others of the melancholy fate of her lover; and also by its having a light at night, visible even in the day time. I thought the story affecting.

On the 25th, we put to sea, and after a five days' passage arrived at Plymouth, having had lovely weather during the time. One day we were becalmed, and the Bay of Biscay was then as smooth as glass, so that some of us put out the boat and bathed in it. We arrived at Plymouth on the 30th, and, next day, received orders to go on board again, as the ship was going round to London. About three o'clock we went on board, and next morning were off Dover, when, being tired of the ship, I took a boat and went on shore. I then took the coach, and arrived in London on the second of September, 1814, and this was no less curious a spectacle to me than any I had been surveying, it being the first time of my entrance into the metropolis.

So now having brought my journal to its final close, I hope something may be found not wholly uninteresting. I crave excuse for some descriptions and impressions that certainly operated powerfully on a youthful fancy. In some instances I have been, perhaps, rather too much captivated with the views and scenery I passed through. I think, however, I can affirm that many were truly sublime, and others grotesque, and, perhaps, unique. However, there is nothing but actual occurrences and surveys which I was an ocular evidence of, and I have scrupulously avoided everything that has even the semblance of fiction.

To a number of readers I must again apologise, who may deem it singular that I should appear so quickly struck, so readily and uniformly pleased with the obvious scenery of foreign landscapes. Let the first early impressions of youth, which, like the other stages of life, has its peculiar modes of expression, be admitted as my excuse. And now, as subordinate to my main design, let me introduce, and embody, in a collective form, some of the occasional observations which I have made, or incidentally prepared for this work.

On a first landing in Portugal, the eye does not fail to perceive and be attracted by the immense size of the convents, which exhibit a sweeping and unconfined range of connected offices continually arresting the traveller's gaze, as it is carried from one line of buildings to another. Of a different character, and adapted to another sense, is that most sulphurous smell which is so strongly felt in the streets of Lisbon, produced by their custom of burning so much charcoal.

As to the civilisation in general of the Spanish and Portuguese nations, the manners and customs of the one form a pretty exact counterpart of the other. A successive intercourse with England for ages has, however, proved the fact, that the Portuguese have a more favourable, or less objectionable, cast of character than their neighbours. I remember a remark applicable to this subject, which had not escaped the attention of a gentleman born in Spain, with whom I was conversing at Biaritz, in France. He observed, and, as I think, justly, that the Spaniards were five hundred years behind the nations of France and England, as to the general result and good effects of an improved and refined civilization. However, to speak accurately, we must draw a line between the superior and lower classes of society, to whom only the remark appertains.

From the lands, both in Spain and Portugal, being so poorly cultivated, we were often obliged to move the troops. Our commissary-general, Sir H. K., an officer of the keenest penetration, was enabled, by a sort of scientific arrangement, amidst the complex involutions of his duty, to provide numerous supplies of provisions, and often where least expected.

The various and prolonged service which made it necessary to order different detachments in different directions, were forwarded with ease, and I do not believe that through the whole war the commander-in-chief was obliged to give up any movement from the impossibility of procuring provisions. The plan which Sir R. pursued, with respect to the account department, was also excellent, but our almost continual marching rendered it impossible for the commissariat officers in charge of divisions, brigades, and regiments, to send in their accounts in proper time.

The Portuguese have a lively air with them, not found in Spain. I had frequent occasion to observe a commendable simplicity in the inhabitants, and especially where our troops had not been before. In many instances, they seemed to feel greatly the attention of our nation towards them, and, with symptoms of good-nature and a fear of offending, everyone would be eager to render us assistance.

The Spaniards, on the contrary, were impudent, and never scrupled to tell us whether they liked us or not. One day after I had paid a Spaniard for forage, a thousand dollars in gold, I put some questions for the purpose of fully eliciting his sentiments as to the opinion entertained by the Spaniards in general with regard to the English. He told me very candidly that the English were not at all liked by his countrymen, although they paid for everything; and the French, who, through the war, had been dreadfully destructive to the countries which they occupied, both officers and soldiers having been the greatest tormentors to the wretched inhabitants, these French, who paid for very little, were held in preference to us. On a general view of the subject, I went on to say that I could not see where the ground of dislike could be, as we were fighting for the freedom of their country. He acknowledged that our energies had been of incalculable advantage to their cause, and that no fault was found with our actions, but our religion was different; we were heretics, and the French were Christians. This cleared up the point, as the whole engine of their aversion turned on this principle.

Those magnificent and durable monuments of superstition, the convents, swarm with friars and nuns almost beyond belief. In any opulent family, where there are many sons and daughters, the heir and eldest daughter possess every valuable advantage that can arise from polished culture or an elegant education; while the younger members are placed in convents. There, however, they are sure to live well, as money is usually given with them. The priors or abbesses of these places live like petty kings, and have an attendance superior to that of many lords. No one can call them to account for their actions, except the bishop, or a cardinal, and the Pope. The best law among them is, that the convents are obliged to admit a number of those who have nothing, equal to those who bring a revenue.

The Spaniards may with justice be censured for that fond madness with which they apply to the gaming-table. Even the peculiarities of the sacerdotal character will not hinder their priests from engaging in such scenes. The police, knowing the pernicious effects of gaming, destroy its implements wherever they find them. The principal game is *Banco*. This I have never played myself, and therefore cannot describe; but I have frequently observed, in private parties, that the little mountain of gold which stood before each person at the beginning of the game, has been transferred to some other person at the close. Sometimes only a few gold pieces were to be seen. None had won; all vowed they had lost; the money had disappeared, but where it went none could tell. This I could very well account for, as I could see the winners now and then slipping a handful into their pockets unnoticed.

The air throughout both Spain and Portugal is very pleasant, except on the mountainous regions, where, in the night, it is as cold as in the month of December in England. When our army reached the Pyrenees, the wounds of many who had recovered broke out afresh, and numbers were sent back to the hospitals established in our rear. At the time our army lay on these mountains, the frost and snow were dreadfully keen and severe.

In Spain there are few gardens to be found anywhere; vegetables are, in general, very scarce, and in many places, not to be had. Carrots, parsnips, and turnips, with a species of small potatoes, are the principal garden esculents. The last are about the size of a large marble, and are brought to the table well sugared. The domestic comforts of dinner parties, prior to the entrance of the English, were almost unknown; but I am informed that this kind of social intercourse has since become very common. While our army lay before Pampeluna, they so gleaned the country of provisions, that, in the winter ensuing, many hundreds of families were literally starved to death.

In the Pyrenees, where lay the scene of hottest action in the guerrilla war, many thousands of the French were annually cut off. If I should estimate their loss, at this one point only, at between two and three hundred thousand men, I should not fall short of the mark. As to what might be our estimate loss, during the whole peninsular war, I am not competent to ascertain; but I think we may allow an hundred thousand for deaths by illness, and for the casualties of war, a number certainly not less.

On our arrival in France, whole fleets of merchantmen had brought from England immense quantities of provisions and necessaries. The little town of Passages, and the banks of the river Adour, were like a fair; and in the little village of Bocault, numberless wooden booths were erected, and shops opened.

Some brokers arriving also from England, a great trade was carried on in shoes, boots, pantaloons, braces, knives, forks, spoons, teapots, shirts, and other articles. Many, I have been told, made their fortunes here, as our pay had been advanced to us, and all arrears due, which were considerable, were paid up at Bourdeaux.

It is impossible to describe the majestic scenery of the Pyrenees; mountain piled on mountain, and rising in tiers, till lost in the distance. Many capped to the very top with trees, others bare rocks. The valleys that lie between are tolerably fertile, but on the Spaniards' side there is little cultivation. The French have every acre in good order, the forests thinned, the underwood removed, and the country in general has a cleanly appearance. One crest, or elevated point, rising over Lozaca, forms a landmark to ships at sea; the top is inaccessible, from the abruptness of its rise, which is many thousand feet above the level of the sea. Through, and among some of these mountains, runs the small river of Bidoessa, near which the French attacked us on the day we stormed St. Sebastian.

LEONAUR

ALSO FROM LEONAUR
AVAILABLE IN SOFTCOVER OR HARDCOVER WITH DUST JACKET

CAPTAIN OF THE 95th (Rifles) *by Jonathan Leach*—An officer of Wellington's Sharpshooters during the Peninsular, South of France and Waterloo Campaigns of the Napoleonic Wars.

BUGLER AND OFFICER OF THE RIFLES *by William Green & Harry Smith* With the 95th (Rifles) during the Peninsular & Waterloo Campaigns of the Napoleonic Wars

BAYONETS, BUGLES AND BONNETS by *James 'Thomas' Todd*—Experiences of hard soldiering with the 71st Foot - the Highland Light Infantry - through many battles of the Napoleonic wars including the Peninsular & Waterloo Campaigns

THE ADVENTURES OF A LIGHT DRAGOON *by George Farmer & G.R. Gleig*—A cavalryman during the Peninsular & Waterloo Campaigns, in captivity & at the siege of Bhurtpore, India

THE COMPLEAT RIFLEMAN HARRIS *by Benjamin Harris as told to & transcribed by Captain Henry Curling*—The adventures of a soldier of the 95th (Rifles) during the Peninsular Campaign of the Napoleonic Wars

WITH WELLINGTON'S LIGHT CAVALRY *by William Tomkinson*—The Experiences of an officer of the 16th Light Dragoons in the Peninsular and Waterloo campaigns of the Napoleonic Wars.

SURTEES OF THE RIFLES by *William Surtees*—A Soldier of the 95th (Rifles) in the Peninsular campaign of the Napoleonic Wars.

ENSIGN BELL IN THE PENINSULAR WAR *by George Bell*—The Experiences of a young British Soldier of the 34th Regiment 'The Cumberland Gentlemen' in the Napoleonic wars.

WITH THE LIGHT DIVISION by *John H. Cooke*—The Experiences of an Officer of the 43rd Light Infantry in the Peninsula and South of France During the Napoleonic Wars

NAPOLEON'S IMPERIAL GUARD: FROM MARENGO TO WATERLOO by *J. T. Headley*—This is the story of Napoleon's Imperial Guard from the bearskin caps of the grenadiers to the flamboyance of their mounted chasseurs, their principal characters and the men who commanded them.

BATTLES & SIEGES OF THE PENINSULAR WAR by *W. H. Fitchett*—Corunna, Busaco, Albuera, Ciudad Rodrigo, Badajos, Salamanca, San Sebastian & Others

AVAILABLE ONLINE AT www.leonaur.com
AND OTHER GOOD BOOK STORES

NAP-1

LEONAUR
ALSO FROM LEONAUR
AVAILABLE IN SOFTCOVER OR HARDCOVER WITH DUST JACKET

THE JENA CAMPAIGN: 1806 *by F. N. Maude*—The Twin Battles of Jena & Auerstadt Between Napoleon's French and the Prussian Army.

PRIVATE O'NEIL *by Charles O'Neil*—The recollections of an Irish Rogue of H. M. 28th Regt.—The Slashers— during the Peninsula & Waterloo campaigns of the Napoleonic wars.

ROYAL HIGHLANDER by *James Anton*—A soldier of H.M 42nd (Royal) Highlanders during the Peninsular, South of France & Waterloo Campaigns of the Napoleonic Wars.

CAPTAIN BLAZE *by Elzéar Blaze*—Elzéar Blaze recounts his life and experiences in Napoleon's army in a well written, articulate and companionable style.

LEJEUNE VOLUME 1 by *Louis-François Lejeune*—The Napoleonic Wars through the Experiences of an Officer on Berthier's Staff.

LEJEUNE VOLUME 2 by *Louis-François Lejeune*—The Napoleonic Wars through the Experiences of an Officer on Berthier's Staff.

FUSILIER COOPER *by John S. Cooper*—Experiences in the 7th (Royal) Fusiliers During the Peninsular Campaign of the Napoleonic Wars and the American Campaign to New Orleans.

CAPTAIN COIGNET *by Jean-Roch Coignet*—A Soldier of Napoleon's Imperial Guard from the Italian Campaign to Russia and Waterloo.

FIGHTING NAPOLEON'S EMPIRE by *Joseph Anderson*—The Campaigns of a British Infantryman in Italy, Egypt, the Peninsular & the West Indies During the Napoleonic Wars.

CHASSEUR BARRES by *Jean-Baptiste Barres*—The experiences of a French Infantryman of the Imperial Guard at Austerlitz, Jena, Eylau, Friedland, in the Peninsular, Lutzen, Bautzen, Zinnwald and Hanau during the Napoleonic Wars.

MARINES TO 95TH (RIFLES) by *Thomas Fernyhough*—The military experiences of Robert Fernyhough during the Napoleonic Wars.

HUSSAR ROCCA by *Albert Jean Michel de Rocca*—A French cavalry officer's experiences of the Napoleonic Wars and his views on the Peninsular Campaigns against the Spanish, British And Guerilla Armies.

SERGEANT BOURGOGNE by *Adrien Bourgogne*—With Napoleon's Imperial Guard in the Russian Campaign and on the Retreat from Moscow 1812 - 13.

www.ingramcontent.com/pod-product-compliance
Lightning Source LLC
Chambersburg PA
CBHW032056080426

42733CB00006B/301